GAMBLING HOUSES

The Eight Quarter Journey
to Overcome the Emotional,
Mental and Physical Pain of
Default and Foreclosure

ANTOINETTE MARIE ANTONE

AuthorHouse™
1663 Liberty Drive, Suite 200
Bloomington, IN 47403
www.authorhouse.com
Phone: 1-800-839-8640

First published by AuthorHouse 5/21/2007

ISBN: 978-1-4259-9498-3 (sc)
ISBN: 978-1-4259-9497-6 (hc)

Printed in the United States of America
Bloomington, Indiana

This book is printed on acid-free paper.

Thank you for your interest in the Spectrum Covenant Series on housing. This is your form to order your CD/DVD's, become an "Intimate Apparel Partner", or attend an expo or conference. Please check the appropriate box below and make your check payable to:

National HOME Alliance, Inc.

o CD/DVD		$ 9.99
o Expo or conference		$ 29.95
o Community Services Awards Banquet		$ 129.99
o INTIMATE Apparel Partner	(1)	$ 29.95
	(2)	$ 14.95
	(3)	$ 9.95

Send checks to:

10808 Foothill Blvd., Ste. 160,
#107 Rancho Cucamonga, CA. 91730.

Please place this form in your envelope
and check appropriate sections.

A SEVEN-YEAR TREK!

It's January 4, 2007, and it's been a total of seven years since the 2000 inception of the National HOME Alliance program. Our first client was served in 2003. Since that time, the National HOME Alliance has been in operation and on the journey to attempt to provide specialized support housing packages to those families who have credit concerns, who are unable to afford the current housing prices, or who are presently losing their homes due to option ARM (Adjustable Rate Mortgage) loans or other financial products that have proven to be a hindrance to the traditional homeowner.

The National HOME Alliance will provide specialized support housing packages to those of you who need to downsize into a more affordable housing package, those of you who simply want to become an owner for the first time in your life, those of you who have recently defaulted or foreclosed on another home, and especially those of you who are on a fixed income (e.g., social security or retirement).

Best of all, the National HOME Alliance will design a housing package to protect your investment today while providing an inheritance for your family tomorrow. You see, our motto here at the National HOME Alliance is, "Keep America HOME." Therefore, our first initiative is to provide housing opportunities that will propel you toward your desired goals.

We here at the National HOME Alliance realize that the spiral roller coaster of any housing adventure that leads to an unfavorable consequence can be quite draining on a marriage, a family, children, and the mortgage holder. Thus the National HOME Alliance and its partners and members are determined to provide services to a population of individuals who have chosen to take a gamble in the housing arena only to lose the bet.

Do you fit this category?

How can the National HOME Alliance serve your housing needs?

FORWARD WE FALL IN HOMEOWNERSHIP

We individuals of failed homeownership have seen our ups and downs, our twirling and hurling, our screams of terror, our night sweats of mental anguish, and our drama of inconsistent decision making. We who have faithfully attempted to provide the payment to the industry of banks, mortgage companies, and/or investors only to fall off the mark can continue to battle the ranks of understanding while once again becoming homeowners via the NHA! I have found that most individuals who have lost a home in the past have gone on to find an affordable rental and have not attempted the homeownership trek ever again.

One reason for the lack of ambition toward homeownership is that once the credit of these individuals healed from the traumatic blow of the housing loss, the costs of the housing market had gone up too high for the now-ready buyers to afford the payments.

The second reason homeownership may seem impossible is the fear of repeated failure. The fear of failure seems too high of a price to pay, especially as one gets on in years. For these reasons, many individuals have decided to become long-term renters. Unfortunately, there is a major dilemma that occurs from the neglect of making a decision to purchase another home that has been seriously overlooked by the renter.

The consequences of the past have kept these families in a false sense of security by causing them to believe that the housing market will one day drop (as in the 1990s) to a pricing structure that will suit their personal needs. The unfortunate truth is that the housing market has been rising and will continue to rise even in the midst of some small pricing dips. Just ask those who paid $19,000 for their homes back in the 1970s.

My personal advice would be to purchase as soon as you can regardless of your credit, and if you can't afford to put the large 20 percent or 25 percent payment down, then await the first opportunity and contact the National HOME Alliance about their equity share program. Or simply purchase a home within your affordability index. Even if it is a manufactured home, the equity will still be there, and I'm a personal witness to that.

Another uncertainty for many renters is the possibility that their home's owner will desire to sell the home when the housing market increases, thus leaving the occupants in a frenzy to find another rental that could possibly have a higher rent rate. A major finality in housing is the realization that if we don't fight to own a home, there is a strong possibility that we won't retire or have an opportunity to sell our home or pay cash to downsize and live off of the balance like our housing predecessors have done.

Well, enough of the housing woes!

Let's discuss my journey to provide housing services to a target market of individuals who just want a first, second, or third chance at the housing game.

CRAWLING FORWARD

My personal housing adventure has left me seriously exhausted spiritually, mentally, and emotionally. I even had a dream that my spirit man was crawling on the floor toward the finish line, and my flesh man was pushing my spirit man from behind with his right foot toward the destination of housing. Now that's what I call motivating yourself to move toward a goal.

AS MY HOUSING WORLD TURNS

My personal battle to obtain the perfect purchase for our family and seek out new purchases for the National HOME Alliance families that I presently serve seems impossible at most, and I have yet to find housing options that are not increasing in cost dramatically. And the houses that are not increasing come in droves, though they have great costs in location, renovation, and/or clouded titles or property liens.

As my housing world turns, I continue to fight and fall for the perfect buy for each family, and though I have made a dedicated choice to fall forward even when it seems as though I've fallen off a cliff, I still become disillusioned at the cost of housing today. I am sometimes fearful of where the housing industry will take tomorrow's families. Many times I have wondered if or when the housing arena will dictate a new level of poor and rich counterparts, thus eliminating the middle-class population of people.

Speaking of falling off a cliff, listen to this cliffhanger scenario.

Five days from this day, I'll need a total of $75,000 to put toward my park projects that must be titled in the new owner's name per the park owner. On the ninth of January, I will be going to court for the fourth time only to have them tell me to come back in six weeks. As of right now, I need a total of $580,000 in funds to close the projects for over thirteen National HOME Alliance families. And no later than ninety days from date, I'll need a total of $400,000 for a total of five families to take possession of their stick-built homes.

How do you plan to get the funds to complete your projects?

Well, to tell you the truth, in 2006, the Lord provided in ways that only he himself could. Paying refunds, labor board fees, and payroll taxes was an excruciating and treacherous adventure at most. My faithfulness to believe that God has chosen us to complete this task in housing and the prayer that I prayed over seven years ago are still in effect. This leads me to also believe that his covenant to provide for our services will be granted, though in his timing.

How do you know he will provide for you?

"For the eyes of the Lord run to and fro throughout the whole earth, to shew Himself strong in the behalf of them whose heart is perfect (just right) toward Him." 2 Chronicles 16:9 KJV Seeds of Wisdom Topical Bible

BACK IN THE DAY!

In the last section you spoke of court, refunds and the labor board. What do you mean?

Back in May of 2006, my trusted friend attempted to destroy my company, and fortunately for me, God's mercy and grace allowed me to move forward in the things of the Lord, though with great, disturbing, turbulent persecution. I've personally seen the promises of God step into the courtroom on my behalf, provide financial provision right on time on behalf of the company, take vengeance on my behalf, and supernaturally promote me to the next level, all for just remaining faithful to the call of God and overcoming my fears and insecurities for the sake of the housing call.

You see, I've been in situations like this on many occasions since our default back in 2000. My only reward has been to see the Lord's hand move miraculously on my behalf for my good and to his glory.

But this particular season in my life feels different. This particular move of God is as real as it gets. For such a time as this season alone, due to this war bout and because of my faithfulness to trust him and not man, my gracious Heavenly Father has decided that this is the time for my breakthrough! He has truly become my *Bel Periza*, as Jerry Sevell would have put it!

You see, I recently gave a substantial seed to a ministry of God's choosing in order to allow God to correct all of the wrongs in my personal life and business. I beseeched the Lord to instill favor amongst man and God. And in my attempts to fight to the end of this journey to provide specialized support housing to people abroad, I vowed to see it to the end regardless of the persecution, in spite of the verbal attacks, and in lieu of my inability to feel adequate to serve such a program to the people.

My specific prayer was to provide upgrading options for those families who were faithful to the National HOME Alliance. And lo and behold, my prayer was answered☞

(Order Jerry Sevell's *God of the Breakthrough* series and study it.)

☞When you see this symbol, you must contact us to order the following message to complete your assignment (The *God of the Breakthrough* by Jerry Sevell).

DELIVERANCE AT HAND

Now that God is in the process of delivering me from my enemies, and because I have chosen to become an over comer through Christ Jesus and have continued to intercede and stand in the gap for the people and housing, the Lord has supernaturally promoted me, thus taking this company to its next level.

I now beseech you, the people, knowing that one chases off a thousand and two chases off ten thousand. Life itself will continue to bring wars and rumors of wars that we all must battle, so it's imperative that we bind our spiritual forces together and get with one accord and fight with each other and not against each other to win the battle. By doing so, we will eventually conquer the war of housing!

"Herein thou hast done foolishly: therefore from henceforth thou shalt have wars."
2 Chronicles 16:9b KJV Seeds of Wisdom Topical Bible.

JOINED FORCES

It's time to join forces and come together with one voice to continue to provide housing services and initiatives for those of you who still need affordable housing. Our National HOME Alliance magazine, *With One Voice*, will present its first issue sometime this fall.

Will you join me?

We need your personal story for the National HOME Alliance Magazine, which is due for release in the fall of 2007. Would you like to tell your housing story? You will receive a stipend for your story, your time, and your effort, and you will have an opportunity to be heard by many individuals who may be interested in helping you.

Express your concerns about the housing industry openly in our "Speaking Up/Talking Back" section of the magazine. Stay anonymous or mention who you are; it's up to you!

Will you join us?

REACH BACK/PARTNER UP

I'm offering to each of you journalists an opportunity to partner up with me as an intimate apparel partner (IAP) who will be offered opportunities to publish stories about housing woes and who will receive important information via the many successful business ministries and investors within my circle of life that will come to visit with our IAP families. This partnership will help you overcome your housing dilemma more effectively and promptly.

I beseech you to partner up with us—a company that has a fertile ground in housing—and allow the transference of God's favorable, unmerited power to penetrate your current situation while directing you toward a future path that will assist you in reaching a positive end.

Partner up with us for $29.95-$14.95-$9.95 per month and allow God to bless your housing situation, because what you do for others, God will do for you!

Then join me at many IAP special events that are specifically designed for those who see the need for our housing initiatives. May God bless you and keep you, and may his face shine upon you and give you peace.

Now! Let's talk a little about the SPECTRUM Covenant Series.

SPECTRUM PROLOGUE

Hello, my name is Antoinette M. Antone and this SPECTRUM Covenant Series of journals that you are about to encounter is my personal adventure from housing to homelessness to housing to homelessness to housing.

Yes! I said it twice. I know that it seems extreme, but if I hadn't gone through it for myself, I would have never believed it. My prayer is that you will encounter my testimony, embrace it, and learn from it.

Let the wisdom and understanding that I have attained over the years of failure and eventual success lead you into a perfected homeownership experience that is not only suitable for your family today, but is also a blessing to your family's inheritance tomorrow.

DEDICATIONS

I would like to dedicate this journal series to the many people who have lost housing during this perilous time of buying and selling. Thank you for not giving up on me. I will continue to fight to the finish for your housing options, and I will continue to seek out viable educational tools that will keep you secure in your homestead.

I give thanks to those who have supported the National HOME Alliance housing initiative with financial support, time, or effort.

I extend my personal thanks to Lonnie and Wendy Pearson our best friends, who have continued to believe in this program and who have stood in the gap for us on many occasions. Thank you, Wendy, for becoming a SPECTRUM network partner in 2006 when things were being revamped. That took courage and faith, so I bless you. Thank you Lonnie for stepping into the foreman position for one of the alliance companies and doing all that you could to keep us moving forward.

Thank you to Thomas and Marjorie Carter (my parents), who have given all they can to support a program that they believe will be a housing opportunity of the future. Thank you also to Bishop Al Harris and Pastor Janie Harris, evangelist Trish of Men and Women on the Move Ministries of Moreno Valley, CA, who have continued to support our efforts and accept us and propel us into our next level in Christ in spite of all of the battle scars that are apparent. To Pastor Mathis and Mom and Jerrie of New Generation Church of San Bernardino: Thank you for your prayers, support, and belief in the program, and thank you for awaiting the reopening of our doors.

To Mitch Brandon: Thank you for your financial support and believing in us with all your heart and not with your mind; you are truly a friend in Christ. Thank you to Mrs. Emma Frias, who stood by us financially and continued to stand in the gap for us even in the midst of not understanding God's hand on this program.

Thank you to Mr. George Dailey and Evangelist Shellie Dailey of San Diego for teaching us how to enter the threshing floor in prayer and supplication and for financial support for our transportation department. To Terry and Danielle Archer of Mississippi: Thank you for encouraging us during the reorganization of the company and for opening our way into our Operation H.O.P.E. (Housing Outreach Program that Empowers) Butterfly Fashion Shows.

To Richard and LaVerne Antone (our parents): Thank you for believing in us at the beginning all the way through to the end, and thank you for awaiting your investment return, which is much warranted. Thank you to Tom Cook for dedicated support and for awaiting the finalization of the partner buyout and for financial support for our transportation department. To Judy Cuen (Our first senior package): Thank you for allowing us to serve you in the midst of a chaotic partnership buyout.

Thank you to the manufactured housing industry for embracing our program and allowing our options to expand opportunities for clients to obtain homes. I send a special thank you to Mesa Homes (John, Jason and Jim): Thank you for allowing me to purchase my homes for my families at affordable prices. And finally, thank you to Boyce Belt, who saw more in me than what the world presented. I truly say thank you, and may God bless you.

SPECIAL BLESSING

I would like send a special blessing to Gary Stephens for never giving up on us and for continuing the fight regardless of what the outcome may have looked like. Thank you, Gary, for your selfless heart and desire to help those who were less fortunate than you were, God surely looks down and smiles each time He embraces your heart. We love you and say again thank you.

Thank you, Nadine; you know who you are! Thank you for believing in us when times got tough and hard. Thank you for standing in the gap for us. I know that God will bless you greatly for your efforts.

Special Sponsor Blessing: Albert Beck

Finally, I would like to send a special blessing out to Albert Beck, my personal sponsor, who has become a great friend and tremendous asset to this campaign. I thank you for believing in me and pushing me through my own insecurities and for the finances that assisted us in restructuring the buy-out purchase of this program from the existing partner, which led to the reopening of the National HOME Alliance doors. I would also like to thank you for your personal involvement in our efforts to provide specialized support housing to and for people abroad.

PARTNERS, FRIENDS, AND FAMILIES

To all of the program partners, friends, and families: We love you all. See you at the brunch eon in April, 2007. Ricardo Campos, Jovanna Sandoval, Veronica Velazquez, Laurie Trusty, Rashida and Michael Branch, Mr. and Mrs. Krauss, Tammy Smith and Manuel Medrano, Michelle M. Nielson, Mr. and Mrs. Martinez, Martha Valtierra, Kacey, Mr. and Mrs. Alvidrez, Al Beck, Trish, Mr. Beltrans, Lonnie and Wendy Pearson: Thank you for believing in this program and what we have to offer to the people, and thank you for helping us move forward. May God truly bless you for blessing us.

PERSONAL CONTRIBUTE

I would like to show my gracious gratitude to my Lord and Savior, Jesus Christ, who died for all of my present and future sins. Thank you for the Word of God that was given to lead and direct our steps toward our Christ-anointed walk. I thank God for sending his son to die for my mistakes, misunderstandings, and mishaps. I bless the Lord and pour out my alabaster box upon his feet for giving us the Holy Spirit to counsel and comfort us during our journey to perfection in him. Thank you, Father, for never giving up on me, for calling me, for choosing me, and for seeing in me what I could never see. I would like to thank you for sending me a prophet, priest, and king who was perfectly designed for me—my husband

Derek Antone. He completes me, and he is a man of great and deep wisdom. Thank you for our twenty-two years together, our fifteen years of marriage, and the many more years to come. He is truly my best friend, my confidant, my love, my provider, my soul mate, and most importantly, my husband. Thank you, thank you, and thank you for the *he* part of me!

To My Love: I am blessed beyond measure, and I thank you, Derek Antone, for loving me like Christ loves the church, for encouraging me to come home and work on this program, for holding me to diligence and persistency in the midst of my fears, for not giving up on me, and for never, ever, ever, saying "I told you so" when things weren't going our way. I love you, honey; thank you for being my aerie!

What does aerie mean? Look it up and tell me!

I would also like to thank AuthorHouse for the publication of this book and the hard work done by the valet team to lead us in the right direction.

Okay, let's discover the SPECTRUM Covenant process!

The SPECTRUM Covenant ✞

Covenant: Psalm 89:3–34 "I have made a covenant with My chosen, I have sworn unto David (Derek and Antoinette) My servant, My covenant will I not break, nor alter the thing that is gone out of My lips." (Seeds of Wisdom Topical Bible)

"When you get involved with God's Dream, He will get involved with your Dream." Mike Murdock

The SPECTRUM Covenant of God allows us to experience the rains and storms of life with the grace and mercy of God leading us and guiding us into safe havens that provide divine protection, divine provision, edification, and exaltation, as well as encouragement, peace, and the ability to stand in the midst of the chaos.

This covenant promises that our Father will never again eliminate mankind by allowing the rain ♦ to overcome them.

"Verily I say unto you, Whatsoever ye shall bind on earth shall be bound in heaven: and whatsoever ye shall loose on earth shall be loosed in heaven. Again I say unto you, That if two of you shall agree on earth as touching any thing that they shall ask, it shall be done for them of My Father which is in heaven." (Matthew 18:18–19 KJV)

The rainbow in the sky reminds us of his covenant, and I have personally taken this covenant to the next level in my life. I prayed and beseeched the Lord over the rains ♦ and storms of life that continue to battle against my chosen call.

I inquired with the Lord and was given permission to create a SPECTRUM Covenant with him that will provide the same covenant protection that he used to bind the literal rain ♦ against any future destruction of the earth.

I loosed this same covenant over the spiritual rains, storms, blizzards, meteor showers, volcanoes, locusts, and other natural disasters, dreams, or interventions that the enemy attempted to utilize to kill, steal, and destroy the restoration of my past blessings.

The enemy has been loosed from his assignment against the reception of any new blessings and of the gifts on the shelf not yet spoken to for, and all of the obstacles placed in my path that are designed to hinder the fruition of providing special support housing to the people have been commanded to cease and desist from following the path of destruction.

Whew! That says a lot!

But why are you telling me this?

I am here today to tell you that this vow has worked. It has literally brought me from poverty to prosperity, from rags to riches, from poor girl to rich girl, and if I didn't mention rich, I'd be lying to you.

Oh! I must tell you that the riches didn't come through the door that I thought they would, but that they instead came via another avenue in order to provide for the door (of housing) that I thought would bring in the wealth!

Did that make sense?

I sure hope so!

I must also reiterate that just because I mentioned riches, there came a great responsibility with the release of money that most individuals fail to mention.

The position of riches came from exaltation from the lowest of positions to those of the highest in and through Christ Jesus. The test of being able to tithe $200 from $2000 seems to be a reasonable effort. The trial to provide a $2000 tithe to a specified ministry because of a $20,000 income was more trying. When I was required to bless a ministry with $10,000 even though I had bills of my own, it seemed not only illogical, but almost impossible for me to do. But it got harder. Soon I was encouraged to provide a $24,000 tithe to a ministry, and not from a $224,500 income stream that was received, but from a $50,000 loan that was obtained. After reaching that plateau of giving, I realized that the money was fleeting and that funding the gospel was not only a responsibility and mandate, but also a privilege. Now Derek and I see the funds that enter our programs, ministry, company, and home as opportunities to serve God. It is deemed as the highest service, and with it come great, rewarding benefits.

"Bring ye all the tithes into the storehouse, that there may be meat in Mine house, and prove Me now herewith, saith the Lord of hosts, if I will not open you the windows of heaven, and pour you out a blessing, that there shall not be room enough to receive it." (Malachi 3:10, Seeds of Wisdom Topical Bible by Mike Murdock)

We realize that he knows our needs and has yet to let any one of those needs not be fulfilled, and when you truly believe this, you begin to live a lifestyle that propels you beyond the riches.

BEYOND THE RICHES

There is a position beyond the riches that most Christian leaders are attempting to obtain that the layperson doesn't see. And to be honest, very few Christian leaders make it to this point, and those who do are celebrated to the utmost, as were King David, King Hezekiah, and King Josiah, and for our day, Billy Graham. All of these leaders obeyed the commands of the Lord without fail.

Now, there are many other ministers to mention, but for the sake of time, I won't do so. To my amazement, not many kings, ministers, pastors, bishops, evangelists, teachers, ambassadors, or Christian chiefs pass up the tasty temptations set in front of them to make them fall, and thus many of them leave enmity between themselves and God.

Do you know what enmity is?

It is for this reason and this reason alone that this passage of scripture must be a focal point in my life:

"Let the brother of low degree rejoice in that he is exalted: But the rich, in that he is made low; because as the flower of the grass he shall pass away. For the sun is no sooner risen with a burning heat, but it withereth the grass, and the flower thereof falleth, and the grace of the fashion of the perisheth; so also shall the rich man fade away in his ways. Blessed is the man that endureth temptation: for when he is tried, he shall receive the crown of life, which the Lord hath promised to them that love him." (James 1:9-12 KJV)

It is this crown that we should seek and search to obtain. All else, finances included, can come and go at a whim. It is far better to partner up with a program that you believe in than it is to reap the blazing fire that will continue to haunt those who have been chosen by God to pursue high position or rank in Christ.

My God-chosen assignment (housing) and my provision point are merely the testimonies of housing, and I will forever battle within this ground. My battle is for me, my predecessors, and my children's future.

Do you know what your battleground is?

Let's except assignment to propel you!

Oh! It looks like you have a couple of assignments.

✍ When you see this symbol, please answer the question and keep up with the assignment number. If you see four symbols, you are on assignment number four!

✍: Write down all of the provision points that you feel God has given to you to make a living or to provide for your family. Which one are you currently operating in?

✍✍: Look up the word *prosperity*! What does this word mean to you?

The SPECTRUM Covenant has provided to me the greatest assets of all assets: wisdom, knowledge, and understanding!

This, in essence, is the fear of the Lord and being considerate of His way of doing what is right.

If you see this symbol (✎), simply answer yes or no!

✎Have any of you, like me, had enough of the housing woes?

✎Are you tired of being sick and tired of moving?

✎Are any of you ready to be an overcomeer through Christ Jesus in the arena of housing?

✎Did you know that the fear of the Lord equates to purity?

Are you aware that purity simply means to walk in wholesomeness, clarity, cleanliness, and transparency?

Well, that's what the SPECTRUM Covenant journals will help you become: Whole—lacking nothing while seeing things more clearly and precisely as they are. And through your journaling experience, you will be able to clean up your past mistakes, take the test, and literally pass it this time. Learn to receive the gift of transparency by revealing the open-ended story of how God's love, comfort, grace, and mercy kept you and led you to a life that was perfect in him.

✎ Are you ready to receive your purity in housing?

I sure hope so, because we're going to embark upon the SPECTRUM dynamics next. Are you ready?

SPECTRUM DYNAMICS

Let me quickly explain the dynamics of the SPECTRUM and how the covenant is designed to lead you from the first color of the rainbow SPECTRUM to the last.

Let me explain how its design is to instill within you the wisdom, knowledge, and understanding that is needed to overcome the topical study (housing) that is being discussed.

✍ ✍ ✍What is the topical study that we are encountering within this series?

S.P.E.C.T.R.U.M. INTERACTIVE
JOURNAL SERIES

The eight series of interactive journals are offered quarterly. The disposition of this program allows the reader to follow the colors of the rainbow, while overcoming their own personal housing issues. They will enter and exit their own personal spectrum covenant, which will lead them through a healing process, thus allowing them to overcome the intense pains, hurts, and feelings of failure in housing.

Each letter of the word *spectrum* will have a reference point that the reader will be required to focus upon throughout the given sections of this twenty-four-month housing journey. Before we continue, let's answer some questions.

Will it take me twenty-four months to obtain a home?

That's up to you! The points accumulated will determine how quickly or slowly a family receives a home. The key is to get your first journal in, which will establish your initial point system.

What are these points based upon?

That's a great question!

The spectrum point system is based upon your answers to the questions asked within the journals. Those answers that portray honesty and integrity will receive a higher score than those answers that are answered with deception and pride.

Question: How many points can I attain per answer?

Answer: Each question has a point system scaled from 1 point for simple answers to 8 points for answers that require action from the reader. Each journal receives an accumulative point scale based upon the least amount of points one could obtain within the journal to the most amount of points one could obtain within the journal.

Question: How will I know how many points that I have accumulated?

Answer: Your assigned coordinator will reveal to you your point rating and how to score higher. Your coordinator will also reveal to you how or what you must do in order to get closer to receiving help towards your current housing situation.

Question: This journaling system seems time consuming and tedious, why would I choose to go through this program instead of using other methods of help with my housing issues?

Thank you for asking!

The National HOME Alliance offers over 20 different programs specialized to support homeowners who are in need of remaining or becoming successful homeowners. These programs include but are not limited to:

Successful Seniors: The National HOME Alliance especially desires to serve our active adults and seniors with housing packages that make sense. Look at Judy for instance, who was awarded a package worth $346,000 for only $89,000. After the sell of her home, she was unsure of her ability to afford a new home. The National HOME Alliance committee reviewed her information and awarded her the following contract: Her space rent to be paid in full for a 25 year period of time, a housing security system, a vacation package (one location per year not to exceed a total of $3000.), a buy-down of her manufactured home package from $136,000, which provided a savings of $42,000 off the cost of her ordering and placing her home within the community. Judy has a future option of obtaining a counseling contract for the children serviced within the National HOME Alliance families. (Must adhere to rules and regulations and qualify for any/or all programs or housing packages)

Majority Medical: The National HOME Alliance had the opportunity of supporting a medical professional with an opportunity to remain within 55 minutes of her work place while providing a safe place to live for her two young adults. Veronica a single mom who was awarded an upgrade housing package to a four bedroom, 2.5 bathroom, 2000 square foot home within a gated community from her manufactured home. And though there was very little equity within her manufactured home due to drop in the housing market, the package was still accepted. Mrs. Veronica handled her manufactured housing package with integrity and responsibility thus making her eligible for an upgraded package. Veronica accepted an Equity Share package, which provided a 20% percent down payment and a monthly payment assistance of $1288.00 per month for the life of the contract. Veronica will pay a mortgage share of $1000.00 per month and receive a vested equity share of 40% percent of the future appraised value of the property. (All National HOME Alliance programs are non-transferable)

The National HOME Alliance is the bridge over your troubled waters. How may we serve your housing needs?

Now! Let's continue with our SPECTRUM color block

The SPECTRUM color block will indicate the status of quality pertaining to the level of purity (clarity) beginning with the color red and proceeding on to orange, yellow, green, royal blue, dark blue, purple, and ending with violet. As you graduate from block to block, your responsibilities and requirements will become progressively more difficult. This process will assist you in overcoming your initial housing issues, while educating you how to create feasible, obtainable housing goals.

By the way what is our topical goal?

Housing, right!

Now! Let's discuss our spectrum Point of Reference Chart

POINT-of-REFERENCE CHART

The point-of-reference-chart is very simple and allows you to embrace working through the journal in your way and at your own pace. Charting through the SPECTRUM is as simple as 1, 2, and 3; and to make it easier, simply contact your coordinator for tutoring and assistance.

There are five aspects of the reference chart: letter code, reference code, color block, command code, and transparency goal.

The process is simple. When you come to a letter code (such as *S*) within the reading journey, simply go to the reference chart and follow the letter code across to the transparency goal until you have completed each color level. This format allows the reader to graduate through their journey toward the final color of royalty and purity without much effort, and once again, at their own pace.

As you graduate from color spectrum to color spectrum, you will embrace various tasks, responsibilities, and requirements given you by your coordinator that will lead you toward your personal housing goals. It is very important that you remain interactive. This allows your coordinator to coordinate with me and you about your immediate housing needs and future goals.

Your coordinator is responsible for providing the necessary housing paperwork, education coordination, and housing options while assessing and reporting your ability to stay focused and follow directives.

Remember: Our goal is to "Keep America H.O.M.E," so if we can keep you in your current location, that will be the first step, but if not, then you must make a decision to get to another location until a suitable housing solution presents itself.

Can you stay the course? How badly do you want to be home?

Now let's describe the five distinctive points within the SPECTRUM chart.

CHART DESCRIPTION

As mentioned, the reference chart has five distinctive areas. The first is the letter code which is simply the stability point. This is the point that the Lord desires within us. It is his desire for us to become stable in all of our ways. It is imperative that if we need wisdom in any area of our life, we not only ask for it, but also trust that the answer that we prayed for came from God, regardless of the obstacles, issues, hindrances, or persecutions that come prior to the manifestation of the end. We must seek wisdom! Obtain a full understanding and hold onto the knowledge of Christ in order to stay stable.

SEEK WISDOM

"My brethren, count it all joy when ye fall into divers temptations; knowing this, that the trying of your faith worketh patience. But let patience have her perfect work, that ye may be perfect and entire, wanting nothing. If any of you lack wisdom, let him ask of God, that giveth to all men liberally, and upgraideth not; and it shall be given him. But let him ask in faith, nothing wavering. For he that wavereth is like a wave of the sea driven with the wind and tossed. For let not that man think that he shall receive anything of the Lord. A double minded man is unstable in all his ways." (KJV James 1:2-8)

Unfortunately, many of us do not know how or even when to be stable in our mindsets, and though I have personally figured out how to become more stable in my mindset, I have yet to perfect my total mental stability. Fear of man continues to plague my mental caverns during my times of war. But I must not let it! I need to overcome these fears and focus on the things of the Lord.

You, too, will need to grasp all of the mental stability needed to remain focused on your goals in housing or anything that God calls you to do for his kingdom. You must stay focused upon your life's call even when you feel that the answer you have received is not in your best interest. Please, I plead with you to stay focused! Don't let the baby die, as Pastor Janie Harris of Men and Women on the Move Ministries would say.

INTIMATE APPAREL PARTNERS

✞Are you an intimate apparel partner of mine?

For just $29.95 or $14.95 or $9.95 per month, you can have access to my stability point series, which gives detailed information about how to become obsessed with your goal and never give up on the things of God. Any or all information is free to those who will be committed to sending in $29.95 per month to help fight homelessness. Just send us the enrollment sheet located on the first page of your journal.

Now back to the reference chart

REFERENCE POINT! WHAT is That Again?

The reference point is literally the arena of the Lord that is actually occurring within your life at a particular time or season.

Let me explain: The reference point is the makeup of S.P.E.C.T.R.U.M., which is another word for rainbow.

I have noticed that during each major turn of events or happenings within my life, there was a specific process that I had to go through before I could graduate to the next level of knowledge and understanding. The events that were designed to kill, steal or destroy my dreams, passions, and goals, were redirected by the hand of God to teach me good things about him and his salvation. The Lords intervention, allowed me to see that his ever protecting hand was with me all the time and at the end of each travailing moment, I could look back and believe in my heart that he was right by my side. God, through Jesus Christ was able to show me his covenant of love and now I can truly give all of the Glory to God for saving me out of each and every situation.

The spectrum series of journals provides to you, the reader, an opportunity to understand what covenant color you are presently in or entering into. The process from S-Stability to M-Manifestation is simple, but our ability to self-sabotage our own outcome is what causes our blessing hindrances and delays.

This information is vital to your success, but it is only offered to those who will be committed to assisting us in our housing and homeless efforts. As you can see, all great knowledge and opportunities must come with a price to those who desire to obtain it. Sign up as an Intimate Apparel Partner and receive a free signed copy of the first book within the Stability Point Series. (This Book will be available for purchase in July 2007)

The information is in a book of its own that has not yet been released, but for now, I will give you a synopsis of the process.

S.P.E.C.T.R.U.M.

We must become **stable** in all of our ways while discerning (through **perspicacity**) the truth about our current situations; while allowing God to **expose** the good, bad, and ugly through the purging process; and while trusting God in what we do not see by embracing a **credulous** state of mind as he works his miracle power to transform us by making us **transparent** in his presence, thus accepting our **renewal** process, which leads to the restoration of all losses, thus keeping us **unified** in Christ by becoming knowledgeable of his promises, his protection, and his provision in leading us to the **manifestation** of his will in and over our lives, thus allowing all things to be added unto us and giving us pleasure in magnifying his holy name and proclaiming to the world his goodness and mercy.

Well, that's SPECTRUM in a nutshell. Which is your reference point?

✝Can you break down the word SPECTRUM within the above paragraph, define the reference words and identify the statements that precede or follow each word?

For example: C-credulous
Definition: To believe without evidence
Statement: Trusting God in what we do not see

Now back to the reference chart.

THE COLOR BLOCK

This is a unique area of focus. The colors of the rainbow represent many different facets. This section adds a fun dynamic to your daily journaling. It will be your responsibility to contact the National HOME Alliance at 1-800-769-7232, listen for the code, enter the code# in and listen to your color block assignment.

THE COMMAND CODE
And
TRANSPARENCY GOAL

The command code within the reference chart will give you a demand that must be completed in order for the behavior to stop affecting you negatively, and the transparency goal is a spiritual requirement needed to become an overcomeer within the topical study that you are now encountering.

"To him that overcometh will I grant to sit with Me in My throne, even as I also overcame, and am set down with My Father in His throne." (Revelation 3:21 KJV)

"He that overcometh shall inherit all things; and I will be his God, and he shall be My son." (Revelation 21:7 KJV)

✍✍✍✍What is an overcomeer? What does this mean to you? (Look up the word.)

By the way, join us at an exclusive graduation bruncheon dedicated to the graduates of each color block and enjoy learning valuable lessons from fellow journalists about their past and current situations while embracing new strategies of how to overcome future housing obstacles.

Now let's lay out the spectrum points in
housing via the reference chart.

REFERENCE CHART

Letter Code	Reference Point Code	Color Block	Command Code	Transparency Code Goal
S	Stability Point	RED	Stop Behavior Stay Focused Fear the Lord	Psalms 34
P	Perspicacity Point	ORANGE	Look, Listen, Learn Discern All Avenues	
E	Exposure Point	YELLOW	Seek At All Costs	Matt6:33
C	Credulous Point	LIME	Matter of the Heart	Isaiah 11:3
T	Transparency Point	ROYAL BLUE	Mercy Receives Victory over Judgment	James 2:13
R	Renewal Point	DARK BLUE	Be Mindful over the Matter	James 3:13-18 & James 4:7-10
U	Unification Point	PURPLE	NHA Alliance Called to Chosen	1Peter 1, 2, 3:1-17
M	Manifestation Magnification	VIOLET	We are saved We will be saved We are being saved	Romans 10:9-17

Each time you complete a reference section, you will be assigned points that will eventually accumulate to a final number at the end of each of the eight journals. This point system allows the National HOME Alliance committee to monitor your commitment, desire, and ability to follow directions. These series of journals also allows the National HOME Alliance committee get to know how to better serve your specific housing needs.

How does the SPECTRUM point system work?

That's a great question!

Throughout this housing journal, you will see your SPECTRUM point of reference within the basic information given within this journal. When you see (SPR), you should refer back to the reference chart, seek out the letter code (such as SPR-S) and answer the following questions to the best of your ability. (Note: you were already given an SPR-S reference earlier in this journal; however, if you have not completed it, please do so now!)

1. What word does the letter code represent?
2. Define your reference point code.
3. Apply your reference point code to your current situation.
4. Each color of the rainbow has a specific and dynamic meaning. Call the following number to find out the meaning of the color and complete the assignment associated with the color block.
5. Please call 1-800-769-7232 and follow the directions to get your assignment for your color block completed.
6. Apply each command code to your current situation. For example: I need to stop trying to purchase a home that I am unable to afford monthly. I need to stay focused on writing this journal, which is my financial breakthrough provision point. I need to fear the Lord in the arena of tithes and offerings.
7. At the same time, send in all of your answers to your symbols (✍ ✎ 📖📖📖) with your SRP. You will be contacted by an NHA coordinator, and this person will go over your answers and your final score will be given, as well as the responsibilities needed in obtaining an NHA housing package.

📖 *"The mark of the Promise is as important as the Covenant itself" (Derek Antone)*

43

Once you have completed the reference point, please send us a copy along with the answers to any or all questions within the section. Send your responses to:

National HOME Alliance, Inc.
10808 Foothill Blvd., Ste. 160, #107
Rancho Cucamonga, CA. 91730

If you are need of prayer, please call our
prayer hotline @ 1-800-796-7232

THE PERSONAL DAYS OF MY LIFE

Now that you are familiar with the SPECTRUM and its power, which is designed to lead the reader into his or her redemption and covenant walk through the perilous avenues of homelessness to housing and to creating a home in and through Christ Jesus, we can continue on with my personal journey to and through housing.

Are you ready?

Well I wasn't!

And If the Lord asked me to go through all of it again, I would pass out and give up the ghost.

To this day I don't even know how I got through it. My only reasoning is the Lord's grace and mercy and I believe he had to slip me some sanity pills during my sleep quite often.

Okay let me get back on point!

Let's begin our journey by establishing our
housing Foundation:

FOUNDATION IN HOUSING

Now I realize that most of you don't even realize that your foundation has not yet been built. This misconception keeps your family structure from becoming firm and permanent. It is for this reason and this reason alone that you have yet to find your stability point in housing, and truthfully speaking,

"Home Is Where The Heart Is!"

It is important for you to remember that the process of default did not occur overnight, nor will it be an overnight sensation or miracle re-establishment. However, many miraculous events can and will occur as you proceed down the road of housing recovery.

You ask, "How do you know?"

Well, I've been there and done that! I've been there and done that!

Yes! I said it twice.

And even though my housing recovery could have been deemed treacherous, rough, and time consuming, I would like to call it miraculous at most. It took effort, focus, and a willingness to overcome any and all obstacles. At most, I had to become obsessed to obtain the goal of owning another home, and more importantly than that, I had to help others obtain their housing goals in order to reach the housing potential that I felt Christ was leading me to.

Pastor Jamal Bryant stated, "You must be diligent and focused. You can't receive the blessing by standing in a hundred-dollar line, becoming a covenant partner, or giving your neighbor a high-five."

He's right you know!

Many of us have interpreted our ministry teachings to be that we could attend a convention, stand in a giving line, or partner up with an established warrior of God and walk into instantaneous blessings.

Well I'm here to inform you that although the above-mentioned items are necessary in order to remain obedient to the things of God; faithfulness, focus, diligence, and motivation are not the only things required to receive your graduation ticket to the next level. It is, in fact, a mandate.

✍✍✍✍✍By the way! Please stop right now and define the words *faithfulness*, *focus*, *diligence*, and *motivation* and place them in sentences pertaining to your current situation. For example: I must maintain my faithfulness to provide housing to families even when my housing situation is uncertain. To obtain focus within the year 2007, I will read the Word of God on a daily basis. It takes diligence for me to work out each morning and to monitor my health and strength. It takes motivation for me to sit down and journal each day about my concerns in housing.

WARTIME and HARVEST

Remember, we spoke earlier of wars in 2 Chronicles. Well, with every war won there will be a bountiful harvest. I'd like to talk to you about wartime and harvest!

"Be not deceived; God is not mocked: for whatsoever a man soweth, that shall he also reap. For he that soweth to his flesh shall of the flesh reap corruption; but he that soweth to the Spirit shall of the Spirit reap life everlasting. And let us not be weary in well doing; for in due season we shall reap, if we faint not." (Galatians 6:7-9 KVJ Seeds of Wisdom Topical Bible.)

In every event (that I can remember) within my thirty-nine years of living, I have found that each scenario of life came with a war that was fought and won or fought and negated or fought and lost.

During the war, I found that my spiritual skills were either sharpened or exposed as ineffective, but nonetheless, each war propelled me toward my reception of the spoils of war, or in other words, a harvest.

Okay! Okay! Don't beat me down with a stick! I realize that it's supposed to be seedtime and time to harvest, and it is!

I would like to remind you that during your wars, many seeds are scattered abroad that are meant to bring in a harvest. The outcome of receiving the harvest depends upon your ability to stay faithful to the end of the war. Unfortunately, many of us don't stay steady during the final battles within the war, and thus we leave the war and the contents of the harvest. Let's go to the book of Timothy:

"I have fought a good fight, I have finished my course, I have kept the faith:" (2Timothy 4:7 Seeds of wisdom Topical Bible)

Timothy speaks of the fight and of allowing it to run its course. In other words, he speaks of being faithful to the end, which is where the war leaves rewards. Let's go to a Biblical war that depicts the spoils (rewards) and harvest (bring in, gather, return, collect).

"The sons of Reuben and the Gadites and half the tribe of Manasseh went out to war...... "And they were helped against them, and the Hagarites were delivered into their hand, and all that were with them: for they cried to God in the battle, and He was entreated of them; because they put their trust in him, and took away their cattle; of the camels fifty thousand, and of sheep two hundred and fifty thousand and of assess two thousand, and of men and a hundred thousand. For there fell down many slain, because the war was of God." 2 Chronicles 5:20-22 KJV)

After the war, the hand of Christ would try my spoils of war in the fire to see if I was in line with his word or operating in my flesh to obtain the things of the world.

After the trying of fire, Christ would allow me time to let go of bad events or happenings. I would then receive a mandate to let Christ complete the spiritual operation of any or all emotional, mental, or spiritual flaws and ineffective areas of my spiritual walk that either hindered a successful outcome or rendered me useless at one time or another during the war.

The harvest was always available to me but it was not yet released until Christ knew that I saw things through his eyes and not my own. My faithfulness toward the things of God thru his son, Jesus, was tried and tested for purity in my National HOME Alliance adventure, but on many occasions prior to this point, I needed to go through spiritual surgery to see things his way. You see my mental capacity to understand the things of God tended to be hindered by the pain and exasperation of the fight during the war. On many occasions my memory would remain focused on the visual or emotional effects of what I saw around me or actually encountered.

This may not be the case for you, but on various occasions it was required of me to go through a spiritual surgery of sorts in order to remove all of the symptoms, injuries, and effects of the housing war, thus making me effective in the battle that had begun.

I had to remember that through the life, death, and resurrection of Christ and his blood alone could my conscience be saved. It was the only way out of my depressed state of mind.

"How much more shall the blood of Christ, who through the eternal Spirit offered himself without spot to God, purge your conscience from dead works to serve the living God?" (Hebrews 9:13-14 Seeds of Wisdom Topical Bible by Mike Murdock.)

I had to call upon the Master Surgeon to perform a mental, emotional, and physical surgery of sort. I became the patient, who was in fact, patiently awaiting the final outcome of the procedure needed to heal the wounds established during this wartime of housing.

"And He said unto them, Come ye yourselves apart into a desert place, and rest a while: for there were many coming and going, and they had no leisure so much as to eat. And they departed into a desert place by ship privately." (Mark 6:31,31 Seeds of Wisdom Topical Bible by Mike Murdock.)

OPERATION H.O.P.E.

Imagine that your housing situation has knocked you out on the housing table of life and death. You've overpurchased only to find yourself heading toward financial ruins or you've invested in trying to flip a house but only added to your debt and not your income. Maybe you purchased many other homes hoping to utilize the refinance options and equity increases to live on, and now it has caught up with you because the rent rates are substantially lower than your mortgage payments. Perchance you did everything right except for giving your marriage over to the hands of the Lord, and the divorce has left your family homeless and helpless. For the sake of mentioning, you might be the person who decided that you wanted to exceed the Joneses and not just keep up with them, and now you find that you are losing your housing battle because of your equity line of credit. Possibly, you've been forced into an early retirement right after making a major housing purchase. Just maybe, you lost your job, just like me. Nonetheless, any or all circumstances leading you to this particular time in your life have, in essence, left you months, days, minutes, or possibly seconds away from financial ruin. The only alternative is to, through much prayer, find a suitable soul who is willing to relieve you of your obligations or to help you find a job, which would now probably be too late.

Well, that's not so with a National HOME Alliance personal profile. Allow us to provide hope to your situation via our many options, whether it be through an investment strategy or a purchase package. Or, if you simply want to just be involved, then join us at our first annual Operation H.O.P.E. (Housing Outreach Program that Empowers) Fashion Show fund raiser. We'll make it "Fun 2 Raise the Standards." 90 percent of the net proceeds from journals 2 – 8 are dedicated to providing housing packages, programs, and payroll to or for families in need. Don't miss out! Join us!

SURVIVAL OF THE FITTEST

Survival is an opportunity to receive the breath of life through Christ Jesus. But first you must follow his rules, regulations, policies, and procedures manual—which is the Bible—to engulf your heart, mind, and soul with vigor so that you will have the strength to stay fit for the course. And for added success, allow the Holy Spirit to lead you to books or materials—just like this journal that you are reading—that will be deemed necessary to win your battle!

Don't begin to think that the individuals writing books or charging you for tapes and CDs will stop charging in order for you to afford what you need. I, too, had times during which I was unable to purchase necessary items to extract teaching tools needed to overcome particular instances within my life, but as I supported God's kingdom with my tithes and offerings, God provided the necessary items that I needed to understand what I was going through at the time. He'll do the same for you! Yes! He loves you that much!

☉ *INTIMATE APPAREL SECTION*

Intimate Apparel?

Oh! You have a couple of questions! Okay! Let's hear them!

Can anyone become an Intimate Apparel Partner?

The answer is yes! There are three different categories of participation.
> (1.) Ambassador Partner $9.99 per month
> (2.) Teaching Partner $14.99 per month
> (3.) Coordinator Partner $29.99 per month

Each partnership position comes with it various opportunities and benefits. When you send your check to the National HOME Alliance, 10808 Foothill Blvd., Ste. 160, #107, Rancho Cucamonga, CA. 91730, you will receive your IAP Open Entry packet.

What exactly is an Intimate Apparel Partner?

Well, where do I begin?

📖When you see this symbol, you will need to refer to the Word of God for your answer.

The intimate apparel section is a very transparent, personalized time given to partners who need to see deeper into the things of God. Let me explain: Many times during my walk with Christ, I heard pastors speaking of naming it and claiming hold of it, but it didn't work for me. During perilous times in my life, I heard pastors say "Walk on it to possess it," and I did this, but it didn't work for me. On my battlefield of losing my home, I wasn't able to go to the church to say "Can I have my tithes back?" or "Can you help me out now that I'm in a crunch?" On many occasions when I was down and out, I noticed that pastors presented this perfect picture of being saved and sanctified from the pulpit while perfectly dressed and adorned in jewelry, but this wasn't the case for me. At my wits' end, I found it difficult to understand how pastors would seek out tithes and offerings and purchases of their books and CDs, yet not offer some sort of financial help to the poorest people of the church.

You see, I had questions! And the questions that I entertained, only God could answer.

Therefore, I get very intimate with those of you who seek it, and I reveal answers to questions that the Lord himself has instilled within me. It is now safe for me to say that I now know why all of the previously mentioned things did or did not occur, and the answer is simple.

"But without faith it is impossible to please Him: for he that cometh to God must believe that He is, and that He is a rewarder of them that diligently seek Him." (Hebrews 11:6 KJV)

"God never responds to your need----Only responds to your faith." (Mike Murdock Seeds of Wisdom Topical Bible.)

You see! There are principals of God that each one of us must follow, and pastors and ministers are merely the deliverers of the messages that we need in order to be successful. Though many ministers and pastors desire to help as much as they can, they can't have faith for you, but they can intercede on your behalf as partners in your life. Trust me in this! Here are some basic answers that might help you until we meet again.

Q and A

Can I start reading the Bible today and receive the blessings that it contains within it by tomorrow? 📖Isaiah 1:19,20

Can I claim hold of the victory and lay hold of it when I haven't taken time to get to know the author of the Bible 📖1 Corinthians 4:2

Will it be okay for me to obtain the blessing without suffering the consequences of my internal neglect to obey and follow God's principals and precepts in my past?📖 2Timothy 2:2-26

Can I stop the calamity by going to church on Sunday and crying out to God about my situation though I have never offered him the most important thing that I have, which is me?📖Hebrews 11:1-8

Are you living by faith or fear?

These were just a few questions that I too, had at the beginning of this journey back in 1997, and now I know the answers.

Are you an Intimate partner of mine?

Have you decided to fight the good fight of housing and homelessness with me for $29.95 per month?

Join the club of housing warriors and receive the following benefits package:

SPECTRUM Journal each quarter (4 annually). Enjoy our Community Services Awards Banquet for our graduates (1 annually). You're invited to all of our bruncheons (4 annually). Receive *MAC Magazine*, which provides valuable insights about the manufactured housing arena (4 annually). Receive your access code to SPEChat to communicate with me directly.

I sure hope you've decided to partner up with me! I look forward to meeting you! We will be discussing various intimate apparel information within this and subsequent journals, so keep a lookout.

What if I can't afford $29.95 per month right now? Do you have any other options?

I, too, could not afford to partner up with some patriarchs and matriarchs in the ministry world, and unfortunately, this inability to line up caused delays in my blessings.

MY SUGGESTION IS THIS:

Don't miss out, and if you can't send that amount, then it would be good to partner up with a different package. Or join efforts with two or three people to receive the information that you will need to overcome your housing obstacles in a more efficient manner. **(Only one person can receive the bonus package at no cost.)**

NOW BACK TO THE MASTER SURGEON:

Your acceptance contract before surgery states that you have placed your situation in the Master Surgeon's hands. There is a chance that you will not agree to the outcome at the beginning, but you will love the final results. The contract states that you will allow him to remove all gangrenous infections. He has the right to amputate all situations, friends, families, items, attitudes, or things that may hinder your complete healing or total redemption. As the Master Surgeon, he may ask you to attend physical therapy, emotional counseling, or mentality-renewal workshops, or he may simply say "Wait." His final command may insist that you apply no Band-aid to the situation and require that instead of trying to find the easy way out of your situation, you will seek God's face and enjoy the ride to recovery his way.

The Master Surgeon, through Christ Jesus, is available to properly cleanse and stitch our large wounds in finances, housing, family, and marriage, all of which are directly affected by your past and current housing situations. By allowing him to begin healing your hurting heart and renewing your mind with a confidence that only he himself can provide, you must sign the contractual agreement, place your name on the check-in sheet, grab a seat, and wait on the call.

✎ Are you ready for your housing surgery?

The final statement of the contract requires that upon signing, he and he alone can make alterations, changes, hindrances, blockades, or obstacles on your path that may or may not make the contract harder to follow, and if this clause is placed into operation, all previous verbal or nonverbal commands, contracts, or covenants are deemed null and void, and the final outcome is ultimately under his authority. In other words, you were bought with a price and you are his and his alone, no matter the cost to you!

✎ Now, will you sign the contract?

Take the time out to complete the questionnaire section and please send in the answers by photocopying this page and sending it to

National HOME Alliance
18080 Foothill Blvd., Suite 160, #107
Rancho Cucamonga, CA 91730

Questionnaire: ✍ ✍ ✍ ✍ ✍ ✍

✍Are you willing to receive your mega surgery no matter the costs?

✍Does your housing situation need the Master Surgeon's hand, and if so, in what ways?

Do you realize that financial Band-aids will not help this situation? Tell me your feelings!

Are you aware of what you must go through in order to overcome the effects of your downfall?

What are your current concerns about your housing dilemma?

✍Are you currently a Christian?

✍Do you mind being served by a Christian team of overcomeers,

What does Christian mean to you!

Christ's Helpers Rising In StrideTo Initiate Adequate & Necessary Support in housing

By the way, could you take the time to answer the following questions?

✍Are you associated with a particular denomination?

What church do you attend?

How often do you attend church?

✍Do you have a personal prayer life?

✍How often do you pray per week?

✎ Are you a tither?

✎ When did you begin tithing?

How long have you been praying and tithing over your situation?

Oh! One more thing!

✎ Do you attend a Bible study?

✎ Does your family have a Bible study together?

Congratulations! You have now completed the first section of your stability point journal. Please take the time now to complete your SRP-S at this time. ▤ Mail your responses to:

National HOME Alliance
@
10808 Foothill Blvd., Ste., 160, #107
Rancho Cucamonga, CA 91730

SERVICES RENDERED

We are a group of Christians offering services to any or all denominations, colors, creeds, races, religions, and sects. We will not recant our need to serve God. Neither will we be silent about the death, burial and resurrection of our Lord and Savior, Jesus Christ, or deny the supernatural power given to us through the Holy Spirit. In other words, can you or are you willing to accept our hand though it is flawed, though it is unsure of how to serve you, though it is uncertain of your housing end, and though it can never give you all that you need, but can merely point you to the God who can give you all that you need?

✒ Are you willing to let us serve you?

CHRISTIAN SUPPORT TEAM

While you're in the housing recovery room, you will need a Christian support team, which I like to call a CST squad, to assist you in remaining stable and focused throughout your housing journey.

What does the CST squad do?

They will stand in the gap for you and intercede for your dreams, your focus, God's will in your life, and the restoration of all losses while you work through all of your viable solutions, options, and opportunities for your God-given success while you are awaiting your God-chosen position.

Who better to lead you back up out of the ranks of hardship to victory than a person who has failed miserably in business, in homeownership, in credit, in net worth, in friendship, in pregnancy, in weight, in school, in business, in homeownership, in pregnancy, in weight, in friendship, in school, in credit, in net worth, etc. I would repeat it again, but you get the picture.

Becoming successful in business, in homeownership, in credit, in net worth, in friendship, in weight, and most importantly, in my walk in Christ, is a daily duty that I now take very seriously.

SECURED NOT SAVED!

Back in 1997, I came to realize a very important fact about my life. I was not saved! I was secured but not saved! You see, I went to an altar call back when I was fifteen years old. I received the gift of the Holy Spirit by that summer and I proceeded in my walk with Christ. I believed and trusted in him. Things seemed to be going well, but by the age of seventeen, I was pregnant. I was told I could never get pregnant due to an internal condition. In other words, I felt that I could continue to have sex with my boyfriend (now husband) and elude pregnancy. But I was wrong. By the end of the year, I was pregnant. I chose to abort my first and second children due to being homeless. Though I had fought to obtain a scholarship to college, I still did not have a secure place to live. I allowed fear to creep into my decision, and I paid a dear price for it. By the time we were married (I was twenty-four years old), we attended church not for the Word, but for the camaraderie. I had a Bible study at my home every so often to fit in. I wore things that would make a man take a sneak peak. I was unbecoming in public when I was with my girlfriends, but would straighten up when I hit the church grounds. I read the Word of God but I did not believe in the Word that I was reading. I was secured. Secured means protected, held, available, safe, or open to the things of God, but I didn't trust or believe that his word (blessings and curses) were, in fact, true! I, as a matter of fact, was described in the Bible as the following:

"Confidence in an unfaithful man in time of trouble is like a broken tooth, and foot out of joint." (Proverbs 25:19)
"Most men will proclaim every one his own goodness: but a faithful man who can find?" (Proverbs 20:6)
"Moreover, it is required in stewards, that a man be found faithful." (1 Corinthians 4:2)

How can this be?

Oh! It's very common—more so today than any day in the past! Many so-called Christians do not know the Lord on a personal basis. Yes! I said personal basis! They do not believe the Word of God and do not operate within the guidelines of biblical principals, yet they do believe that they are saved, just as I did! And to tell you the truth, I would have never known that I was not saved, had my life not gone down the path that it did! I can say that I am truly saved today and I fight for my salvation on a minute-by-minute basis as if it and it alone is my most treasured possession. This and this alone is why all of these blessings are being added to me! I have made a dedicated choice to seek out the things of God. Would you like to receive the Holy Spirit and allow God to lead and guide your life from damnation and destruction to destination and divinity? Pray this prayer with me!

Prayer of Redemption

Most gracious and heavenly Father, I thank and praise you for allowing me to come before your presence with thanksgiving, and I enter your chambers praising your Holy name, I thank you that you have allowed your Holy Spirit to dwell within your people to lead us and guide us into understanding of who you are so that your ways will be made known to us. I thank you that no sickness of mind or disease of the heart can dwell within me and that all weapons that try to keep me from a full understanding of who you are and your call upon my life are considered null and void. I thank you, Father, that I dwell in the secret place of the most high God and have been chosen to fulfill a life of service to and for his glory. I now receive the precious gift of the Holy Spirit and decree and declare that I beseech that my sins are forgiven me, and I, too, will release pains and hurts done me by others that I may be presented spotless and pure in your sight through Jesus Christ, our Lord and Savior. Amen.

I'm honored that you have chosen to purchase a copy of this journal, thus allowing me to coach you and walk with you until the Master has mastered the new you. I feel this is a privilege in and of itself. I'm thankful to have been chosen by God to go through the battles in various arenas in order to show others their ways out. I look forward to working with the hurting hearts of many of you, and I expect that all who seek the counsel of the Lord and adhere to his teachings will not only be successful, but also fully restored.

It's only through the grace of God and the obedience to make better choices and clean up the mistakes of my past that I have encountered a renewed mindset about my homestead, creditability, and stability, thus allowing God the opportunity to restore and replace all of my losses.

God doesn't look at your mistakes; he focuses on your motives.

The best advice that I can give to you today is to be steadfast and unmovable in your goal to overcome any and all obstacles that plague your success in becoming a homeowner. Most importantly, see each obstacle as an opportunity, not a crisis (though it may feel as such for a moment).

Also, eliminate any venture, so-called friend, or hindrance that would keep you from reaching your designated destination. If the relationship was meant to be, it will return in due season, and the blessing of it will bring no sorrow with it.

Finally, it is very imperative that you throw all of your timing mechanisms out of the window. Don't focus on the time or even the days or months; you have now graduated to seasons.

Jesse Duplantis said, "God wear's a wristwatch, but it doesn't have an hour, minute or second hand. God's watch reads *due season*."

Jerry Sevell repeated that to me in his "God of the Breakthrough" series.

TIMES AND SEASONS

I, just like many of you, have encountered various failures during my journey of obtaining another home. During this season it has been very difficult to stay focused. And on many occasions I wanted to give up.

Well, I implore you not to give up!

Just get started on your plan of action regardless of where that merger begins. Don't be proud. Stop! Look! Listen to and learn the essential keys of success from the many mentors that God has partnered you up with, and open your eyes to the truth that is designed to set you free.

Now join me, and let's learn together how to stay focused!

But first let me get intimate with my apparel partners by asking that you stop reading this journal now and enter the SPEC chat room to discuss the following topic.
Code #Schat010107

"The Illusion of Greatness leads to Prominence"

For the rest of you, please continue to read through the interaction section to obtain knowledge about how and where to begin your personal journey toward housing.

If you are in need of prayer, please call the
National HOME Alliance hotline
@
1-800-769-7232

INTERACTION JOURNALING
The Stability Factor
In Housing

Join me and learn valuable insights that will protect you from making decisions that will hinder your future opportunity of owning a home and becoming a homeowner.

What housing situation are you in presently? _____
_____
_____
_____
_____

Encounter the spectrum series with an open mind, a teachable spirit, and a hopeful heart.

Throughout my journey, I have come to realize that most people are purchasing homes out of their emotions and not out of their foundations. Yes! Here's that word again!

So before we go any further, let's investigate seven key principals needed in building a solid housing foundation.

"SEVEN FOUNDATION PRINCIPALS IN HOUSING"

Principal #1: **What is your salary foundation?**

This is the most important foundation principal because though many of you have been taught to name it, claim it, and walk on it to possess it, you have not continued to research the dynamics of wartime and harvest.

Yes! I said wartime and harvest!

The Word of God says: 📖 *"For even when we were with you, this we commanded you, that if any would not work, neither should he eat." (2 Thessalonians 3:10)*

Your war is in the works, and many of you have a misguided understanding about labor. *Labor* is not living off of your equity line of credit. *Labor* is not owning an empire of homes that you can't afford, refinancing them, and living off of the proceeds. *Labor* is not owning a business that cannot financially support your living conditions.

You must have an income base that God can use to bring in your income to support your investing, your home, and your lifestyle.

I tell you the truth!

There is not one place that you can go where you can say that you will pay it by faith and they will give you your purchase; however, you can have faith in God that he will make provisions for you and your family through some income-related means to make the purchase.

Therefore, I call the next principal the provision point.

Principal #2 **What is your provision point**?

What is a provision point?

This flipside of the faith stance is that God will honor your faith to obtain your blessing via the income base that he has provided for you, even if the actual funds are in the manifestation process. Let me explain:

My first housing project of three manufactured homes on land was a financial means to the purchasing of my mobilehome. Though the financial blessing was not to be manifested for some time, due to building plans and projections and completion of the certificate of occupancy, I began to seek to purchase my mobilehome when God instructed me to, regardless of not having the proceeds from my project. God had showed me my provision point, thus leading me to obtaining the goal of owning a mobilehome. Of course this is just one example of many.

Prior to the provision point coming to fruition, I continued to obey the command of God to seek and search for my mobilehome. I prayed over other mobilehomes that I never moved into. I prayed over land only to see others build upon it. I prayed over developments only to see other families move into them. I continued to fight toward my provision point though the battle seemed to be pointless, and during this time I witnessed God providing for my family in miraculous ways time and time again.

Why did God provide for you during this time?

"He that dwelleth in the secret place of the most High shall abide under the shadows of the Almighty, He shall cover thee with His feathers, and under His wings shalt thou trust: His truth shall be thy shield and buckler. Thou shalt not be afraid of the terror by night; nor for the arrow that flieth by day; Nor for the pestilence that walketh in darkness; nor for the destruction that wasteth at noonday. A thousand shall fall at thy side, and ten thousand at thy right hand; but it shall not come nigh thee. There shall no evil befall thee, neither shall any plague come nigh thy dwelling. For He shall give His angels charge over thee, to keep thee in all thy ways." (Psalm 91:4-7, 10, 11. Seeds of Wisdom Topical Bible, by Mike Murdock)**

Mike Murdock says so eloquently, "Protection Is Produced Through Partnership."

THE PRESSING OF THE WINE

In my attempts to obtain a home, I moved on and forward toward the fruition of my provision point. I was many times disappointed, and sometimes disillusioned, but I was eager to not give up on the things of God. And though things weren't working out my way, and though little understanding followed my effort at the time of my seeking, I fully understand now that the only successful venture is the one that is completed.

I looked and prayed and looked and prayed until God finally said, "This is your home. This is your season of stability."

Getting home takes work—homework. (Purchase Martha Muzzini's CD and play "This is your Season" and "Say the name.")

The following questions are specifically designed for my intimate apparel partners, who support the ministry of housing with $29.95 per month. These questions will be discussed in detail and answered at the next intimate apparel bruncheon, which is scheduled for July 2007.

Intimate Apparel Partners
Send in your membership fee of $29.95 today to
The National HOME Alliance
@
10808 Foothill Blvd., Ste., 160, #107,
Rancho Cucamonga, CA. 91730
Look for your invitation in the mail.

We will get intimate about the things of God. Transparency will be the key factor, and any question asked will be answered in order for my IAPs to grab hold of their blessings sooner than those who are not under such counsel. Don't miss out. The majority of the funds obtained by the membership will be utilized to support housing or home-ownership initiatives, so bring your testimony.

Now here's an excerpt of one of our open discussions:

Our bruncheon topic will be:

What exactly is a provision point?

Here's an excerpt of the last question:

What kind of problems did you go through
while trying to obtain your goals?

WARTIME IN HOUSING

Wartime: In October 2005, the Lord inquired with my husband and I to step out in faith and provide housing to a current National HOME Alliance member, by giving them a package on our mobilehome. After much debate and fear, we set out on the journey to own a "stick built" home. We set out to find an Option to Buy purchase and to our dismay it failed miserably. When I placed my house in escrow, our company was going through the most treacherous test I had ever encountered. We were being accused, required to refund buyers, asked to remove our clients from a park, and forced to give up our office, among other terrifying events. As the Lord informed me to move forward and purchase another home and offered the one that I was in to my best friend, we hesitated and set out to do it. The house was already in escrow and all the payments were paid on schedule. Nearing the end of the escrow, our funds were delayed by 10 days causing the original owners to become hostile toward our escrow completion. One day we came home to find a for sale sign in the yard and when an inquiry was made, the owners stated that we could remain in the home until it sold or close our escrow earlier. We opted out of our escrow and moved out before our next payment was due. A few months later, we noticed the address on the foreclosure list. The house was in foreclosure and that's why the owners were trying to press us for an earlier close.

By the grace of God, one of our clients could not perform on their package on the day their keys were given to them, so we took possession of the home on a (12 month) lease purchase and we are closing this loan as we speak. But prior to the close of the loan, the Lord again asked us to move on and upgrade a family that needed a home, after much despair and anger, we followed our faith to another lease purchase only to have the same foreclosure issue occur. We were devastated to find a Notice of Trustee's Sale on the door. We placed the house in escrow and entered our lease agreement through a very well known and reputable Real Estate Agency. Were we acting in faith or foolishness?

I questioned him and asked him if he had chosen the right person for this task. I was uncertain of my calling, my Christianity, and the feasibility of purchasing at a time like this, and my income was in a staggering cycle of work and no work due to the allegations. In other words, purchasing a home really seemed hopeless. And to make matters worse, my income seemed to come to a complete stop during the escrow. I couldn't pay my bills for about three months, thus causing some credit concerns, nor could I come up with the security deposit. Our lack of income (due to project delays) should have affected our purchase, but instead of focusing on that, I beseeched the Lord to tell me about the alternative and where or how I could purchase a home, and I wanted to know that I was the owner, and the door opened; it was the perfect buying opportunity for us. But as we are all well aware, too much is given, much is required, and I needed to help two other families get into their homes before I received mine.

(The continuation of this story will be at the April 2007 bruncheon.) For now, let's answer some more questions!

Why did God allow all of that to happen when he asked you to look for your home in the first place?

Here's the answer:

I believe that God asked me to purchase my home during this chaos for two reasons and two reasons only:

(1) To give glory to God for being able to obtain a home without worldly reasoning

(2) To show me his personal goodness toward me for my obedience and my attempted obedience in moving forward regardless of my fears, anxieties, insecurities, hurts, pains, or tantrums. (And this act of faith actually became the faith stance that I needed to be an overcomeer and have the hand of God move miraculously over my situation.)

It is imperative to give him glory and honor before the manifestation, which is the major key to the receiving of the blessing.

How do you know if you're really hearing from God?

I would say that you find out through a confirmation of spirit!

Prior to my blessing, I encountered a wartime, and my harvest could only manifest through a stable mindset and through my remaining focused on the gift to be given by God. I desired financial stability and housing permanency, but was I willing to stay the battle until the end of the war? More importantly, was I willing to go and accept that which God desired for me?

During the wartime in your housing situation, you must stay focused and remain stable in your commitment that the house you will obtain will meet your needs and not your desires, that it will be within your household budget, and that it will be located in an area that fits into your immediate income range.

Now what you didn't hear me say is that the first house you choose will be the house God has selected for you to obtain. What I will say is that you should not stop looking, hoping, or working toward the goal until God says you're finished. Stay flexible, because in the end of the journey, God will bless you with the desires of your heart, but only if you stay the race.

You see, though I have not moved into many of the homes that I thought I would move into, I did receive the most gracious gift of all—an upgrade into a community that I felt that I could afford but did not deserve. The Lord directed me to the perfect location, the perfect price, the perfect sell, and the perfect buy within perfect timing, and it was the perfect opportunity for my future potential as a contractor. It is literally a gem! We are in love and can't wait to take possession of our pearl.

Did you become angry when things didn't work out in your timing?

Well, anger is a natural consequence of feeling denied our flesh, but my inner wisdom reminded me that though I didn't receive that particular blessing when I wanted it, awaiting a blessing made just for me was not only an honorable option, but it was also desirable. But could I stay in the battle and wait out the war?

Would I allow my anger to hinder the arrival of my ultimate blessing, or would I see this as a test from God regarding my faithfulness rather than man's attempt to keep me downtrodden?

> **May I interject a question right now? Why is it that most Christians pout their way out of their final blessings when things don't go their way? Doesn't the Word remind us that we fight not against flesh and blood, but against principalities and rulers of the darkness and spiritual wickedness in high places? Do we actually believe the Word, or is the Word convenient for beneficial purposes only? What if God said no to you about homes you were looking and searching for?, Could you continue to fight and believe? If God told you to purchase other families homes prior to you receiving your own, and if what he eventually gave you did not look as prominent or was not as new as that he had you get for others, could you trust in him and lean not on your own understanding and in all your ways acknowledge him so he could direct your steps? What are you willing to give up for others in order for God to provide for you?**

In other words, your reaction to your current circumstances is your choice. Wisdom would say that you should trust God for the appropriate outcome.

How do you know that what you are praying for will come to pass?

I can only give you my story. So be there with us to be encompassed by information that will only be offered to my most intimate apparel partners (IAPs).

Now let's get back to our principals.

What was the first principal? _____

What was principal #2? _____

Principal #3: **What are you expenses and expenditures?**

Please take the time and write out all of your expenses, and write down any extra things that you might purchase without thinking about them under your expenditures lists. This section is the most important of all, because it will assist you in the establishment of a monthly budget. Contact you coordinator to receive a faxed copy of a National HOME Alliance budget sheet. if you need some help figuring out where or how you spend money ask your coordinator for assistance.

Principal #4: **Do you know your FICO credit rating?**
The most important part of your budget will be based upon your buying power. Your buying power will be directly related to your credit score and your income.

For example: An excellent score will give you more buying leverage. (You will not need to place as much money down to purchase items.) A lower credit score will require that you have a capital base to offset the risks of the investor or banking institution. But credit does not necessarily keep you from buying a home.

But what if I don't have money or credit; then what do I do?

Do you have a seed? Tithe into some fertile soil and seek God for an idea or witty invention to generate capital, a job, or an opportunity.

Principal #5: **In what timeline or on what date do you feel you will be ready to purchase?**

It is imperative to understand the dynamics of timing in your purchase. Many people today have purchased outside of their timelines. If they would have waited for a year or two, or even a couple of months, the pricing structure would have been situated for an excellent buying opportunity. Over the years, I have also noticed that many individuals purchased homes out of the pricing ranges right after a marriage or getting a new job, only to have challenges in both of them. This happened to me in 1994 with my job, and if I had purchased the investment property instead of the homestead property, we would have been just fine financially, with or without my job.

Take the time right now to grab a sheet of paper and give me a quick scenario of your current situation. With this information I will help you establish an appropriate timeline for your purchase that will keep you in your home.

Principal #6: **Running Numbers**

What is running numbers?

That's a great question!

It is imperative that each individual take time out to run the numbers of his or her household in order to solidify a decision about the purchase that he or she is embarking upon.

Complete the full budget projection and place the housing amount into your mortgage area that you deem a possibility.

Now, it's apparent that most individuals can't afford even the most basic housing packages today, so that's where the National HOME Alliance comes in.

Let us help you determine where you are today and see which National HOME Alliance package fits your scenario, but prior to receiving your National HOME Alliance package, let's consider the following three key factors in running numbers.

There are three key factors that you must consider about your income today and your income tomorrow. I call this section

FACE THE FACTORS (3):

☺**FACE THE FACTOR about your INCOME(#1):** Consider your yearly income, not your monthly income, as your buying base. Base your purchase on 50 percent of your gross income and then divide by twelve. This will give you a baseline to use in determining your household expense budget.

For example: At $120,000 per year, divide by two, which totals $60,000. Divide this by twelve. You would have a $5000 household allowance.

And I reiterate—household allowance, not mortgage allowance.

Allocate these funds toward all of your monthly obligations and no more. You must remember that your gross income minus your tax rate will probably only leave you a monthly net income of approximately $6600 anyway. With $5000 becoming your usable income, that would leave you $1100 to place in an emergency fund for hard times.

☺**FACE THE FACTOR about your MONTHLY ALLOWANCE (#2):** If you know that you have a monthly household allowance of $5000 per month and you set out to purchase a home for $375,000 at 6.5 percent interest, your principal and interest payments will be approximately $2375 per month, leaving your taxes and insurance at approximately $600. When added to the payment, this leaves you with a total of $2975. You still have more than enough to pay other monthly obligations in a timely manner, and thus you will be building your credit rating. Speaking of credit:

⊗**FACE THE FACTOR (#3) about your CREDIT RATING:** Everyone knows that credit ratings can inhibit or contribute to your purchase. There are those circumstances in which you must get started on a strategy that will propel you into your future goal regardless of your current credit situation. This is where my testimony comes in.

What credit circumstances are you in today, and what is your twelve-month recovery goal?

My Story

It was 1991. I was looking to purchase my own home, and I sought out some fixer-uppers to acquire. I had job stability, and my payments were perfectly aligned with my income. I inquired with the wrong people and was told not to buy the house because it was older than theirs. Though I didn't care about the age of the home, I respected the person telling me, so against my better judgment, I did not start the escrow process. Soon I found a home in good standing that wasn't too old, but another discouraging comment came from a respected friend, so I again negated the purchase. Many years later, the truth revealed itself and I found out that this person was not speaking in my best interest but was, in fact, seeking her own emotional justifications. Where did I go wrong? I listened to someone who had no desire to help me but who wanted to make me look the way she desired to have me look. Soon, after much ado, I made the wrong move and overpurchased. Here's the story:

It was 1994, and Derek and I were very excited to close our first home and move in. I had just been made permanent as a probation deputy, and Derek (my husband) was working full-time at his warehouse job. We were making a substantial income, and our debt-to-income ratio was awesome. We took possession on January 25, 1994, and by September 11, 1994, we were devastated. Do you remember the Orange County layoffs? Well, 10,000 people lost their jobs. I was lucky by being able to keep my career, so I was very happy, and I looked forward to continuing my career goal of becoming a CEGU unit psychiatrist. Soon, the pyramid scam came into play, and I was asked to testify against many people who had ten to forty years of tenure. Though encouraged to lie, I didn't. I told the truth and paid a dear, worldly price. I was harassed, mocked, provoked, and nearly killed, and I soon found myself out on stress leave via workers' compensation.

When I attempted to go back to work, I found out that the "black list" was as real as a cup of coffee in the morning. My career was gone! I was in and out of tumor surgeries, I had lost our children in miscarriages, and I was even more devastated than I had been. I told the truth! I had been taught that the truth would set you free, not condemn you. I was torn in two when I found that not to be the case. Life went downhill for me mentally, physically, emotionally, and financially as my 805 credit score fell and my home was headed toward foreclosure. I felt betrayed by the world, bitter toward God, and disillusioned about my future. I was afraid of what the future would bring, and I didn't even know how to start over. I just wanted to cry and die! We filed bankruptcy to try to solve our problem, but to no avail. We eventually lost the battle, but by the grace of God we won the war. You can too, you know! God loves you so much that he will restore all of the losses, and his only requirement is to believe that Jesus Christ died for your sins and rose again to redeem you unto him.

GOT CHRIST?

Call us 1-800-769-7232!

Let me teach you how to attain prosperity, and may god also delight in you!

Now, the profession above is not going to be as easy as many-get-rich-quick programs profess. At least it wasn't for me. You will need to make a quality decision to stay focused and not give up. You will need to learn and listen to strategies that will propel you into your success zone. The greatest adventure you will ever encounter will be the one from poverty to riches and from homelessness to homeownership. I guarantee you that!

The difference is that I'm right here with you. I'm not going to give you a book and say, "Follow the instructions, and may the best man win."

I won't have you come to my meetings so you can pay me to give you insights on how to become a millionaire. I will not ask you to purchase my books, tapes, magazines, booklets, and journals and hope that you will read them, complete them, or even understand them.

What I will ask of you is to partner up with me.

I am asking for your help to help you!

Let me use your testimony as you move from level to level.

Let's build a trust between the both of us.

A trusted friendship, if you must!

Let's see if we could be faithful to the things of God, while being faithful to one another.

Allow me to serve your needs and bring you to the next generation of housing stability.

As you test the waters of the National HOME Alliance, I'll try the Spirit by the Spirit and help those who desire to be helped and not those who still desire to be held.

> 📖 *"It is better to hear the rebuke of the wise, than for a man to hear the song of fools." (Ecclesiastes 7:5)*

> *"Parasites want what you have earned-----Proteges want what you have learned." (Mike Murdock Seeds of Wisdom Topical Bible)*

How are you going to try the Spirit by the Spirit?

That's a great question!

This covenant of journals will be the starting point. I will use this activity of mine to determine whether or not I should provide intervention, help, or continue to let the weather beat against the stony heart of the man in chaos.

Many of the nuggets that I have obtained from Mike Murdock's series have instilled my life with wisdom and will become very useful in separating the wheat from the chaff within this housing initiative.

Let me show you how to tell the world that it's okay to believe in the Word of God again. I will introduce you to my best friend, my confidante, my Lord and Savior, Jesus Christ. I will require you to follow the instructions that he provided to all of us. And most importantly, if you will be true to yourself,—never leaving or forsaking your God-given call upon your life—I will allow the Lord to use me to transfer his miracle power into your life for his glory and your good.

Now that sounds all good and dandy, but realty must speak clearly to you, that life is not a bowl of cherries. You must first find the land, till the dirt, plant the seed, water the seed, speak life into the tree, pick the fruit, clean the fruit, prepare the fruit for your meal, and most importantly, eat of the fruit to receive strength and stamina for the endurance of the race.

So now that you have a great understanding of the process that it will take in order to get you up and out of your current situation, why don't you tell me what particular situation you are in? _____
_____
_____
_____

How did you get into this situation?_____
_____
_____
_____

What have you done to get out of the situation?_____
_____
_____
_____

What are some of your options for getting out?_____
_____
_____
_____

What do you think I should do to help you?_____
_____
_____
_____

Why do you think this way?_____
_____
_____

Points of Caution

Thank you for accompanying me through my own personal journey in housing!

Wait! One more thing: Please stay alert while reading this book; this is not a traditional reader.

The purpose of this journal is to intrigue you with thought-provoking monologues and dialogues that will keep your housing goals moving forward.

Caution: The answer that you may be looking for may not be the one that you receive. However, the answer will be the one that you need.

Word of advice: You didn't get in this situation overnight, nor will you miraculously wake up, hear a word from God or receive a point of reference from me and be an overcomeer in housing, but each step that you take toward your own recovery will allow you to take your rightful place in housing and will ultimately provide you a peace and freedom that money itself could not purchase.

Have you received your
play along CD or DVD?

Hello, friends. The next section of this journal has a CD/DVD that must accompany the reading section. Please take the time to send in the first page of your journal in order to register and receive your CD/DVD within the mail.

Within This section you will find details that portray the antics of my life in housing and homelessness. Listed below are all eight covenant series title journeys that you can look forward to. Enjoy!

Avoidance/Denial Syndrome

Enjoy the journey of three girlfriends who embrace housing woes from a very unique perspective.

Tonie is a homegirl from the block who is headed out of the ghetto and into a better life, but in order to obtain a better life for her earthly flesh, her inner spirit man, Chayi'l, must lead and guide her into a personal relationship with the Lord, and thus the battle between her flesh man (for position in her life) and her spirit man (for reign over her life) begins. All the while, her conscience man, Antoinette, tries to make sense of the "me, myself and I" (tri-part) being and how all of us fit into this world, which has so much to offer yet nothing to offer worth losing our souls over.

The entire tri-part relationship begins its battle from within while trying to maintain the balance of serving the Lord while living in a world of chaos, raising a family, working for a living, obtaining friendships that are lasting and permanent, and lastly, following the rules and guidelines of the biblical principals of the Bible in the midst of worldly policies and procedures.

Sounds exciting, doesn't it?

Send for your CD/DVD today! Send $5.99 to:

National HOME Alliance
@
10808 Foothill Blvd. Ste. 160-107
Rancho Cucamonga, CA 91730

If you are an intimate apparel partner, simply send your code number and one will be sent at no cost to you!

Now let's enter the SPECTRUM Network adventures in faith in housing. But first, let's take a look at the next eight quarters in journaling.

SPECTRUM JOURNAL COVENANT SERIES

On homelessness, housing, and building a home!

Hello, I'm glad you've made it this far in your journey.

The following information is the subsequent journals that will assist you in your journey through housing.

And just to make things easier, we here at the spectrum Network Agency, have compiled a topical series specifically designed to coincide with the original journal series. These topical journals relate to specific behaviors and incidents noted within the specific target market. The topical journals are:

Order a Topical Journal for your family or friends:

Fostering by Faith
Prepare for the Game......eliminate the gamble

From the Group to a Home
Life is a gamble........housing doesn't have to be
Adopt a plan of action
Life accepted........Gamble denied

The senior advantage
Second time around.......Housing! No more a gamble

Reality Real Estate
Redemption guide from the perilous effects of investing

Pre order begins May 15, 2007 – July 15, 2007

The first series within your housing covenant journal coincides with your stability reference point. So take time out right now and reflect back on the covenant questions in the reference point section. Our focal point will be concentrating upon becoming stable in our housing projections and options. It's imperative that we renew our thought processes about our housing capabilities and opportunities prior to making a move into our home.

December 1993–1994   **AVOIDANCE/DENIAL SYNDROME**

Red series I   "Dinner With The Marshalls", "When Life Runs Amuck!"

Take a sneak peek at the second journal covenant series, which is due to be released in July 2007. Enjoy more adventures in my housing journey and listen to some inspirational testimonials from some of my most intimate apparel partners and learn what being tried by the fire really means and learn how to utilize what is left from the blaze of fire.

December 1994–1995   **"READING BETWEEN THE LINES OF FIRE"**

Orange series II   "Life's Cookbook Testimonials"
"Consequences Of Eating A Bad Meal"
"Living With Mistakes Or Asking For Mentorship"

I've noticed that most families will do all that they know how to do in order to keep their home except for finding a job at McDonald's or Burger King. can remember riding my bike to a job in a suit with a briefcase in order to meet the needs of my home. When the family finally becomes exposed to the elements of homelessness, the decision to work a second or third job will be too late.

December 1995–1996   **EXPOSED TO THE ELEMENTS**

Yellow series III   How do you decide to stand firm and stay in your home?

During my adventure of finding work, trying to keep my credit up, attempting to purchase a home, negotiating with the IRS, and applying for educational loans, I came to find that obtaining another home was not impossible, but it would take a major decision to find out how I could afford to purchase another home. How can I keep my income up with the growing market? Should I start over in a new career and re-evaluate my options? How do I start over? I'm nearly forty; where would I begin?

December 1996–1997   **MISTAKE MAKEOVERS**

Lime series IV   When should you throw it all out and start over?

Throughout my life, I learned that journaling has kept me in touch with my thoughts. It helped me to investigate what I was feeling or going through at particular points within my life. Over the next forty days, take forty of those days and write down some daily things that may help you to remain focused or simply get your feelings out on paper. Join us at the July '07 brunch, and let's take time to reflect on some of the things that we have learned about ourselves. Use this section wisely and dedicate it to the lord!

SPECTRUM 40

Forty days of change—Asking for favor and grace to allow you to withstand the heat and come out firm.

During my adventure in housing, I made some grave mistakes that could have been fatal, but I cried out to the Lord as a refuge, and now I can give him the glory, as he worked things out for my good. What things do you need for the Lord to work out in your life?

DECEMBER 1997–2001
Royal blue series V

IN THE HEAT OF THE NIGHT

When your own decisions bring on the heat but God gives you a 360-degree turnabout

Obtaining my spiritual freedom was the first goal in obtaining all other blessings. Though this process did not take place overnight, it was worth each day and night of prayer, fasting, and travailing. The path to this freedom came from my remembering verses within the Bible, nuggets from prominent people, and wisdom principals from mike Murdock. All of these things helped to propel me to my next level. What propels you, and what verses do you know?

DECEMBER 2001–2003
Dark Blue series VI

VERSES! REMEMBER THE VERSES

Salt in the water vs. salt of the world, Heat makes you limp vs. heat makes you firm, Staying in place vs. falling forward

GO DOWN FIGHTING

One of the hardest and most humbling experiences that I have ever had was when I confessed to the mess. Even if I felt that the mess was not necessarily my fault, I still took full responsibility for the chaos and proceeded to make attempts to honor my word to each and every person. During this time many of my words were hindered or haltered by spiritual attacks, devilish antics, and/or wicked activities. I could have been disillusioned and placed blame elsewhere and given up, but I'd been down the road of giving up and giving in after much ado before. (And I mean much is due!) The best fighter in a battle is one who goes down fighting and leaves the end result to the Lord! Don't ever give up on anything, and I mean that!
December 2004–2006

WHO'S RESPONSIBLE FOR THIS STACK OF DIRTY DISHES?
Purple series VII

> Fess up to the mess up, a Faith bout to the Cleanout, The Great (I am) Escape, Messup to Miracle, chaos to Creativity, Payup to Praiseup, Kingdom giving = Kingdom living

Did I say due? I really mean due now! I have never been more terrified than when I have owed people money and I truly get the concept that one should owe no man, but should love him. You're gonna love this section of the journey, which details my entire life from poor to rich and examines why I believe god needs me to be financially well to do his will, as he does you!

DECEMBER 2006–2007 **DANCING WITH THE CREDITOR WOLVES**
Violet series VIII

> Bill Blunders, Credit Card Concerns, The big Debt Divide, Tax Troubles, Payroll Problems, Housing Hoopla, fashion flaws, but at the flip of a coin, when you Flip the Script, Fold Back the Covers, Up the Antes

You can start cleaning up now or let all of the chaos continue to pile up. You've got to get up to clean up. You must stay up to pull up. Keep your faith up to measure up.

HOUSING PRELUDE

Life today is difficult enough without having to worry about our ability to provide safe, affordable housing for our families. Let's examine some past information that will give us an idea of where the housing arena is going and how we can join the game of homeownership.

Just four years ago, a median-priced home in Riverside and San Bernardino counties was reported to be $178,440 by the California Association of Realtors. Today the median price is $367,500+ in the same counties.

Each decade, housing becomes more costly, more difficult to obtain, and believe it or not, easier to lose.

The Inland Valley Dailey Bulletin reported, "The fact that the state legislature continues to make it tougher to build homes will dictate that the middle class in California will not be able to buy a home. The rich will be able to buy homes, but the middle class and the poor will not."

We can see this happening today! How much further will the housing market push out the little guy from a housing buy?

As you encounter my adventure, keep in mind that "we have grace for the race," as Perry Stone would say.

Remember: There are two ways to learn, Mistakes and Mentors, which class will you be in. I got that little nugget from Mike Murdock's wisdom series.

Did you know that the housing industry has nearly eliminated the affordability index?

Back in the early '70s, as houses were going for the whopping price of $56,000, Lewis homes offered an affordable package specifically made for the lower-income families. The homes were priced at

$19,000+, and the qualifiers had to prove their inability to afford other housing, and they had to have good credit and an income.

Today all of the affordable housing is priced too high for lower-class families and for some middle-class and working-class families, and if affordable housing is found, it will be on the outskirts of a rural area, leaving those who are already poor no option for getting to and from work.

Listen to this statement found in the *Inland Valley Daily Bulletin* dated Saturday, August 17, 2002:

Bill SB910 and AB680 never made it out the legislative boxing arena only to be beaten down in the fight. Senator Joe Dunn, D-Santa Ana, was the author of the bill's and stated, "the state's lack of enforcement power is precisely the problem," he continued to say the easier penalties (for a county not offering affordable housing options) would "neuter" the bill, letting cities easily avoid their share of (affordable) housing." The bill died in the fight and the reason why is that it reflected complexities of making cities do what their <u>residents</u> often don't want to do - - make room for <u>poorer residents</u>."

The article continues to afford the still-rising median housing price of $319,000.00 and the 56 percent home ownership rate, which is one of the nation's lowest percentages ever. Mark Stivers, a Dunn aide, stated, "communities will continue to flout the law and frustrate the development of housing of all types that we desperately need."

This is why "The National H.O.M.E. Alliance," needs your consistent help in raising funds to change legislation and provide affordable housing options to families. Our purchasing packages are non traditional and are specifically designed to coordinate a purchase for the buyer that is unprecedented.

Let's do it for our housing today, and help us fight for our children's housing options tomorrow and most importantly,

"Let's keep America HOME."

THE DEFAULTED COMMUNITY

I can remember when we defaulted on our first home and sought out options for housing. We became frustrated and disillusioned as we found that there were no options for families whose credit was in disarray due to mortgage default status.

You see! Even though we sold our home prior to the foreclosure sale, we still encountered a great credit crisis, which left us with us no suitable housing options. Mrs. Kirby has firsthand experience with this housing woe.

"The Daily Bulletin excerpted on Monday, August 19, 2002, a statement from Teresa Kirby, executive director with the Aletheian Christian Foundation, said she foresees large numbers of former recipients turning to agencies like hers for utility and housing assistance. She also foresees bigger problems. Mrs. Kirby states, "I think we're going to see an upsurge in homelessness."

She couldn't have been more accurate in her predictions.

I am grateful to begin to address people like you, who are like me and who are in need of someone like me to reveal to you how to beat the odds of affordable housing and homelessness. Whew! There, I said it!

That says it mildly, but you get the picture! Don't you?

Now, let's walk through this adventure in faith together and learn from each other. But first, let's take a look at the United States deficit and how it could affect our future home-buying strategies.

On September 6, 2002, Governor Gray Davis signed a $98.9 billion hard-times state budget that made $9 billion in cuts and trimmed the state payroll by 7,000 jobs, and this was one of the latest budget signings in California's recorded history.

On March 28, 2006, I had the opportunity to watch the Blue Dogs (Democrats) vs. the Official Truth Squad (Republicans) in a debate over the National Budget. It was very interesting to learn that 52 percent of our national debt is controlled outside of the United States.

That's right! The majority of our national debt belongs to foreign countries. That's a scary thought!

It was further explained that, at present, if each man, woman, and child were given a $28,000 bill that was due today, it *might* cover the deficit. If I'm not mistaken, the National Deficit is at $2 trillion 23 billion.

How does this affect me, you ask?

That's a great question!

Well, the economy was stimulated by the lowering of interest rates, which caused a false sense of prosperity by allowing sellers to receive exorbitant returns for the resale values of their homes, thus creating many false illusions of riches. Some individuals utilized their funds correctly, and many others did not.

This false evident return provoked non-investors to become investors by purchasing several properties for so-called low-leveraging high returns and flips, but the young investor was focused only on the profit and not the possibility of failure.

This economic jolt also allowed individuals to buy more house than their incomes could afford due to the 50 percent debt-to-income ratio utilization, the ARM flexibility, interest-only loans, and such products as these.

Back in the '60s, the original debt-to-income ratio numbers established were designed to protect homeowners from possible default. Today the mortgage products offered bear witness to constant failure. Maybe we should go back to our original 32 to 34 percent debt-to-income ratio and eliminate the stated income options.

It was also noted that this new proposed wealth from real estate ownership led homeowners to proceed into real estate ventures without proper exit strategies in place for possible flipping delays or rental property mishaps.

During this year alone, several bad deals have come across my desk in which the owner has been in over his or her head. One such case is that of a realtor who ventured out and purchased an investment property His mortgage payment was $800 more than the rent rate. Every time the tenants were late with the payment and ordered a stipend via the National HOME Alliance (Mortgage Assistance Program-MAP), the grant request and seven-to-ten-day processing delay caused the owners great distress, but it was better to have a sure thing than an empty property. Unfortunately, most homeowners can't wait through the delays and end up making a "permanent decision about a temporary situation," as T.D. Jakes would say.

Another young couple purchased a fixer-upper to live in and found that they did not have the money to replace the entire electrical system. They made attempts to option-to-buy the property to one of our National HOME Alliance clients, but the deal faltered because it did not pass inspection.

This couple was stuck with a home that they could not afford, and they did not have an exit strategy to service the needs of the property. The National HOME Alliance attempted to pay directly for the electrical issues, but the owners wanted a direct payment, which could not be given until the issues of the property had been solved and the inspection had been passed.

How do I know this?

Continue to read this series and you will come to understand the one thing that I, too, had to learn: All things worth having take effort, patience, time and stamina; there is no such thing as overnight success, not even in real estate. Not even the lottery brings peace to its winners. The only security you have in obtaining a successful homeownership venture is to learn from mentors or learn from your own mistakes. Which way would you like to go?

Has anyone thought of what will happen once the building industry pace dwindles?

And I'd be the first to tell you that the building industry has not hit its low as of yet! My personal predictions state that the market will continue to sell for the next three years (from 2007 to 2010).

About that time the market will take a terrible dive, and this dive will outlast the infamous 1990–1999 housing woe.

I believe that in early 2007, we will see a piranha pool of people purchasing the new homes on the market possibly because of low interest rates and substantially lower prices, as well as, thousands of dollars in concessions offered to the buyer for the purchase of homes. All of this will stimulate the fish pond once again.

After three years of this, we will once again reach a plateau, and enter some amazing housing adventures.

My concern is that many families will start to migrate out of the state during this time to find affordable housing solutions, and many will end up in Texas, Arizona, or possible further East.

After the twenty-year ploy, the housing industry will once again bounce back and supersede the imaginings of what we thought housing prices could ever reach. I personally inquired about this to the Lord in prayer and was granted a dream, and the outcome was not too nice. But if you don't want to believe me, then you didn't hear it from me!

I'll reveal this dream within a later journal to my most intimate apparel partners.

What are some of the other woes that we can expect due to our California housing adventures?

Has anyone addressed the concerns of the many realtors, contractors, escrow workers, title company employees, and other industry workers who will be caught in the same housing dilemmas that their current jobs helped to initiate?

Don't write me and take that personally unless it should be taken personally!

Many families have been hurt due to being sold homes above their means, and I personally know of one instance in which a woman on social security was sold a $700,000 home because of her impeccable credit. Within six months she was homeless and her credit was gone. She lost her social security because of her purchase, and now she's submerged in a living status that only God can help her out of!

What's your story? Would you like to enter it into the National HOME Alliance magazine? The first edition is due for release in the late fall of 2007.

Where do these individuals find jobs once the industry stagnates? Even if the price lull doesn't fall as far as it did during the '90s real estate dip, the housing default and foreclosure rate will climb to all-new heights. In other words, we haven't seen anything as of yet!

Many of my realtor friends had opportunities to purchase low-priced houses with their income to become investors. Unfortunately, many of them are begging buyers to take over due to the high mortgage-to-rent ratio, and these actions have kept their households in the red.

Listen to Dian Hymer, the author of *House Hunting*, who reiterates the highs and the lows of high-leverage buying. She does inform the readers that using as little money as possible to purchase is wise due to the earning potential being greater if you place less money in a deal. But she also warns by saying, "Keep in mind that where there's a high profit potential, there's also high risk. Leverage works wonders as long as property values are going up. But, when values reverse direction and decline, a highly leveraged investor can end up owing more on the property than it is worth." Ultimately, she encourages a buyer to purchase a home for the long term.

I, Antoinette Antone, say that if you have the right information and an exit strategy that propels the investment into a future bank account, then you're on the right page. Well, I'd like to remind you that you must remember what game of real estate you are actually playing. Learn the appropriate rules of engagement, and most importantly, play to win!

Let's take our example from sports: Everyone understands that the rules of the game vary per sport. Take, for instance, the games of football, basketball, and baseball. There is no way to convert the rules of one of these games to play another; however, it is evident that the dynamic of teamwork is needed to win in each of the games.

How about the athletes who may run track or enter the sport of gymnastics? They, too, differ in procedures, rules and action, yet the dynamic of speed is required to succeed at both.

The aspects of the real estate industry are segregated, just as the aspects of the sports industry are. Basketball, track, baseball, football, and soccer can be compared to investing in home ownership, manufactured homes, multiple-housing duplexes, housing developments, community investments, commercial properties, syndications, real estate investment trusts (reits) or rentals.)

Though the housing industry and sports are very different, we can draw the conclusion that it takes the same stamina to build a home as it does to run a race.

To be a winner at anything, there are some common rules that are universal whether they apply to sports, housing, life, or personal goals:

You must play the game to win. Even if you lose, you must play to win or not play at all.

The playing field must be accurately chosen based upon your ability to stay focused and to utilize your talents.

You must practice, practice, practice, fail and fall, fall and get up, and meditate on the win to become perfect at your game.

You could do all of the above, or you can hire a trainer, mentor, or someone whose been there and done that to assist you in the development of a Plan of Action and Exit Strategy for your course.

RULES OF ENGAGEMENT FOR YOUR COURSE

Rule # 1: Stay alert and vigilant for sections within this journey that will help you answer questions that you may have about housing and homelessness.

Rule #2: Stay on course. Do each series in order and each chapter in its sequence. Find more answers to questions at the journey's end.

Rule #3: Alterations to the course might cause delays to your final outcome; be very careful.

Rule #4: Any deviations to your course might cause unnecessary mistakes. Stay focused!

Case in point: Mistakes cost time, money, and unnecessary energy. There's only one resource in the world that is irreplaceable—time!

Rule #5: You'll hate your mentors in the beginning because they will not give in to your woes. You will be pushed past your fears, so expect to stay focused and initiate your confidence in what you cannot see so that at the journey's end, you will love the results.

Rule #6: Following instructions will not always be easy, but it is necessary in order to graduate to the next level of the housing game.

Rule #7: Stay focused. You'll only reach your ultimate goals if you fight the right battles. If you make your own goals your battle, you will never achieve a positive end.

Rule #8: Don't give up on Christ or on your goals or yourself or on your course of action. This course was designed to get you to the next level, but it takes your own energy, time, and finances to climb the mountains and hills of housing displacement. The National HOME Alliance will review your efforts and accommodate you for them. The harder you fight the greater the assistance. The National HOME Alliance is merely assisting you in obtaining your goals, they are not paying your way to your goals.

And remember:Quitting is not an option!

Remember: a new beginning is just one minute away.

TAG ALONG INTERACTIVE STUDY

The Tag Along Interactive Study is a fun, comparative, adventurous faith walk encountered by Me, Myself, and I. This section is designed to enthrall your senses and keep you motivated to see your situation through the hands of God. Hello, intimate apparel partners. Enjoy the interaction chatroom and receive your code number after the purchase of your first journal.

As you become an alliance member of the National HOME Alliance, your name and story about homelessness could end up in one of the journals as a friend to the characters portrayed.

Now, here are some basic rules for following along with the story.

Follow along with the designated storyline:

(*) story a (**) story b (***) story c

All storylines are created to get you closer to your goal, and each subsequent story allows you to follow and participate in the next journal series.

SEND US YOUR STORY

If you're homeless, have housing concerns, or need to make a house a home, send us your story. If your story is utilized in the next series, you will be contacted so that your story can be added to our *Feature Families* DVD series, and as an added bonus, your story will be added to a journal and you may be eligible to receive royalties for your story.

This interactive series serves as a daily journal designed to account for your own housing concerns, dilemmas, and woes, which may be pressing hard on your spirit and leading you into depression and/or mental chaos.

ADVENTURE DISCLOSURES

Many times during my adventure, I was required to take two steps back in order to take one giant leap forward. At first I despised these setbacks, but I came to realize that they were all parts of the growth process.

THE CYCLE OF SUCCESS

Just as you need to complete eleventh grade in order to go to the twelfth; just as you need to past tests in order to graduate from high school to college: just as you need to face failure to embrace success; just as you must attend your classes, study, and do your homework to pass the test to graduate to the next level, grade, or class: your adventure, as well as my own, can be compared to completing medical school. It takes time, diligence, patience, and self-control to be called a doctor, and God bless you if your desire is to be a brain surgeon.

Are you ready for success? Are you really ready?

All obstacles in your way are designed to make you jump higher, endure longer, run faster, pray harder, plan more effectively, and fight forward.

"Failing is not an option," as T.D. Jakes would say!

Finally, don't give up on your course. You must work out your own salvation with fear and trembling. You'll find that in the Good Book.

What do you mean, "What good book?" Haven't you heard of the Bible?

"Therefore, my dear friends, as you have always obeyed – not only in my presence, but now much more in my absence- continue to work out your salvation with fear and trembling, for it is God who works in you to will and to act according to his purpose." Philippians 2:12-13 New International Version (Rainbow Bible)

Well, Are you ready?

So let's get on with the story.

AVOiDAN(E/DENiAL SYNDROME

*Hello, my name is Tonie. My best friend Chayi'l and I will be escorting you through our adventures of faith in housing. You'll have a chance to here my personal story of faith, flops, and unshakable stops. I betcha you're gonna love the ride. So let's get started.

Tonie: Let me take you back, back, back in time. Not really; it wasn't that long ago. Okay, for real now! Alright, alright! I'll stop playing around. Chayi'l, tell them the story. Go on, girl, tell the peeps the story!

Chayi'l: Tonie, must you talk like that?

Tonie: Girl, I'm just tryin' to be real.

Chayil: It's December 1994, approximately two years after Derek and Tonie got married. She and her husband began to look for a home since he and Tonie both had promising careers. They were ready to settle down and start a family. Well, let me let her tell you about it. Tonie, tell the people what happened.

Tonie: Well, we decided we would accept extended drive times and move to the high desert in order to find affordable housing. This was a promising thought at the time, and it seemed to fit our future goals to become business owners working two companies side by side to provide some sort of affordable housing. Derek was approximately fifty minutes away from work (one way), and I was one hour and eight minutes away (one way) in traffic.

> As I look back, my dreams of yesterday are manifesting today. What were you thinking of years ago that are coming to pass today? Put in writing with the date and time in your journal section.

Tonie: The concept of purchasing a home in lieu of going on a honeymoon came from the fact that prior to marriage, I had lived

106

in twenty-two different places, so purchasing our first home and becoming stable was not only a goal, but also a relief.

As a child, I was hoarded from city to city, and state to state, which left me and my siblings in and out of motels, ghetto apartments, and foster/kinship care systems, and on many occasions, we were homeless.

At the tender young age of six, I began to endure homelessness due to my mother's mental illness disease of schizophrenia.

By the time I was fifteen years of age, I sought out the help of Christ in order to get out of the depression of living and life. And my high-school life was a constant battle of insecurities and hostilities. I was popular and despised, just as I am today.

Let me stop right here and explain my popular/despised statement! It's 2006, just after the holidays, and I'm still fighting the effects of the betrayal of my best friend earlier this year. Let me take you back into the history of the national HOME alliance in order for you to embrace understanding. When the company opened its doors to the public in 2003, I met a friend, and she knew a lot of people who needed to get into homes. You see, my husband and I had encouraged an investor to work with other individuals like us who had lost everything in order to get them into mobile homes, which are one of the most affordable housing arenas provided today. We moved into our first mobile home, sold it when the market went up, and purchased two more—one to live in and another to flip. It worked. eight projects later, I began working with the friend of mine I mentioned previously. The problem started when we began helping people out of our emotions and not out of our wits. I did not embrace the fact that they may or may not fit the parameters of our program. My desire to serve an industry of people who were homeless due to financial distresses misled me from trying all of the individuals by fire to see if they had faithfulness to pay their debt. These individuals didn't qualify for traditional lending, but I still attempted to serve them the best way I could, which would have been just fine had we tried them in fire. We placed our first family in the community in an affordable home via a lease/purchase, which is very common within the industry. In fact, after speaking to many of the banks, I found out that they really didn't care who paid as long as they got their money. So I set out to find more of these projects that could be paid for with monthly payments instead of large down payments or full cash options only. My exit strategy was to complete three manufactured homes on land and utilize the proceeds to outright buy the homes within the park, and my timeframe for the purchase was twelve months. We would then keep the notes and become the lender, thus providing more flexibility than traditional banking industries.

So far, so good! Or so I thought!

Soon it got out that we had helped several families, and our orientation meetings were filling up with at least sixty people per week instead of one or two per week.

We began the three projects in the high desert of San Bernardino County and opened up an office in Rialto, California on May 15, 2005. We hired a construction company to complete the projects, and had about ten projects going in the parks. Our partner at the time decided that we shouldn't use the escrow company that I had chosen because of the cost, so he decided to find his own, but it was to no avail. During that time, we continued to move forward, and we finally made a decision to use a local mobile-home escrow company. Things started to go wrong from day one, but what do you do? Do you keep moving forward or stop in your tracks?

I set in motion three lease/purchase contracts to be paid for within one year. We had an investor willing to pay us $180,000 until the land projects were completed to pay off the loans on the houses and get them titled in our company's name and the new owner's name. We initiated the lease/purchases, started the monthly payments, placed the clients in the homes, and monitored the accounts. Five months later, the $180,000 in funds still had not manifested.

We had a partner meeting to find out if we should move forward or not, but we had no choice but to move forward being that the possession of the homes had already taken place.

Were we on our way? Was it a good idea to do the lease/purchases? Well, you'll find out in the next journal series. Stay tuned!

Now back to me, myself, and I.

During this perilous teenage time of my life, the Lord sent me a guardian angel to help me fight my battles.

Tonie: I was fifteen years old, and I and two other girl friends prayed on campus for husbands that we could have for a lifetime, and do you know I saw one of those girls at the Koinonia Conferences (here's a plug—these aregiven yearly by Life COGIC under the direction of Pastor Ron and Lavette Gibson), and she, too, is still married to the same husband, but that's a whole other journal series that we will embrace later.

Tonie: Girl, let me tell you. I was sixteen years old, and there he was—gorgeous in stature, and his complexion was high yellow. He was an absolutely beautiful specimen created by God just for me! But why in the world would he choose me? I was long, lanky, and my gums were larger than my teeth. I wasn't a pretty sight, to say the least.

But to my surprise, the Lord said we would be, and thus we were, twenty-two years after that tender, young age of sixteen. I'm actually proud of that, and you'll hear about it in a later series, but for now, let's get back to our topic: homelessness and housing.

My husband, Derek, was stable in all his ways. He had lived in two locations during his entire life. He, unlike me, never had to make a grown-up decision for himself, and all major decisions in his life came at the assistance of his mother or father. I remember loving their *Leave-it-to-Beaver* lifestyle.

I, on the other hand, came from a family of businesspeople. My father owned his own construction company, and my aunts, uncles, cousins, and sister worked in the prison system. I used to say that if you weren't in prison, you worked in them. That was my family heritage. Two of my relatives went on to become wardens of some of the most notorious facilities in California, and my maternal grandfather and grandmother owned three group home facilities.

But to my dismay, none of these businesses stand today. I can remember sitting at my dad's drawing table while visualizing the day when I would help him run the family business. I can remember working in the hot sun on the rooftops of houses and plastering stucco.

Did I dare dream?

> **Have I pushed my own goals off on Derek, or have his "Stable Mable" ways entwined themselves into my "Frantic Freddy" thought patterns? Do you have a stable life or a frantic life?**

Well to say the least, Derek and I were as opposite as opposites could be, yet we were totally in love with each other. You see, he completes me, and I him. He is everything I am not and then some, and I love him for that. Though sometimes he can work my last nerve into a frantic fit, I love him and thank him for who he is. By the way, remember that I said this, because you'll question me later in another series about marriage. I guarantee you will!

Wait a minute! I'm way off base! Chayi'l! What is my topic? Marriage!

Chayi'l: It's housing, Tonie! Stay focused on housing and homelessness.

Tonie: Oh! Yeah! Okay, okay, okay!

Tonie: Girlfriend, like I was saying, we had goals, sweetie—a real plan of success—and we were excited to get started.

What we didn't understand was that entering the course and road to success that we would have to take in order to reach our final destination would betreacherous at the least.

Let's get back to the story!

Derek and I decided to focus on business. So where do we begin? How do we get started? What's the first plan of action?

Back in 1993, we located some excellent starter homes that were just over $50,000. Our decision was to move into one, upgrade one year later, and continue that process until we reached the goal of owning five or six homes. Our goal was cautiously thought out and placed upon a plan of action, and we set out for implementation.

As we devised a plan and started to put it into action, our final idea was to ask someone about it, but we chose the wrong counselor.

What an exciting time for us! But one day we proceeded to speak to this person about our desires only to be told not to do it and that we should not dream so high! To this day, I'm not sure why we asked this particular individual, but what I have learned is to watch the counsel you set up under, and I tell you that from the heart.

Our plan was on the way—or was it?

It was January 1994, and our home-buying plan had gone drastically off course. We had moved into a much larger home. Yes, I said moved. I would like to tell you that we contemplated our decision, sat down and discussed our options, and made a quality decision based upon our family design and future goals, but I'd be lying out my teeth, and though my teeth are little, the lie would not be.

In reality, we listened to the voice of some family members and woke up the next day and signed a contract for a 3,010-square-foot home. To be exact, we've decided to stay in this home for at least thirty years and move only if we want to.

Chayi'l, I really don't know what changed our plans.

Why did we stray from our original plans?

What caused us to become so unstable in our thinking, and why didn't we stay firm?

Do you need to answer these same questions?

Tonie: There I've said it. I feel easier. I blew it. I've made the wrong decision. I should have stayed focused, but I didn't.

Chayi'l! Do you have any suggestions to help me figure out where I botched it?

Chayi'l, how do you remain so focused on your goals to the point of accomplishment?

Why did you reach your goals and I struggle for one successful day to follow the next?

On many occasions I awake afraid of the day.

Tonie: You're no different than I, Chayi'l! We're the same age. We have the same taste, and many of our goals are similar, if not exactly the same, and the only thing different between us is the fight against flesh and spirit. I fight against my spirit on a daily or minute-by-minute basis, and you die to the flesh on a minute-by-minute basis.

Tonie: What's wrong with me? Why am I such a failure? I hurt on a daily basis because I still have not reached my goals, and many people have been hurt deeply by my pursuit to help myself to help others! I'm tired of not liking me! I most of all hate awakening each day, looking in the mirror, and saying, "I don't even like you!"

Turn off the camera; I feel like crying!

Chayi'l: Tonie! Tonie! Wait, wait. Turn the camera off; give her some time to compose herself.

Chayi'l: Well! Here she comes. Are you okay?

Tonie: Yeah! Well anyway, as I was saying, how did you become so successful Chayi'l? And how can I learn from your success?

Chayi'l: Come on! Come with me! I want to introduce you to someone.*

This ends storyline A*. Please take a minute to complete the assignments within the boxes prior to completing your reading. Write all of your answers in the journal section of this book and don't forget to make a copy of your answer page and send it in to me for analysis. I love you dearly. Stay focused and keep up the good work. God is watching our stability right now. He is instilling constancy, steadiness, firmness, strength, and permanence in our spirits to help us stay the race.

Now back to the story.

Chayi'l: **Let's go visit Sir Wisdom to inquire about your first point of instability. Grab your bike; it's a ways away.

Chayil: Whoosh! Here we go!

Chayi'l: Watch out! Duck! Look out for that tree! Hey! Wait for me; I can't pedal any faster.

Tonie: Well, keep up!

Chayi'l: Watch out for the windy road, and don't forget that it's—

Tonie: Downhill! Oh No! Help! I can't stop my bike.

Chayi'l: Tonie! Try using your brake!

Tonie: Too late!

Sploosh!

Tonie: I'm good, girl!

Chayi'l: Are you okay?

Tonie: Yeah! The lake stopped me!

Chayi'l: Tonie, didn't you see that brake pedal on the handlebar?

Tonie: Oh! That's what that is. I saw it, but I didn't know how to use it.

Now back to the story!

Tonie: Chayi'l, help me out of this messy water.

Chayi'l: Wow! You're drenched. Would you like to return home to change your clothing?

Tonie: No! I don't have time. I better go as I am.

Chayi'l: Okay then! Tonie, the door is right over there.

> Well let's go. Are you sure he can help someone like me?

Tonie: Well, go ahead; ring the bell or something.

Knock! Knock! Knock!

Sir Wisdom: Yes, who's there?

Chayi'l: It's me, Sir Wisdom. Me—Chayi'l! And I've brought my best friend, Tonie. Can we come in and visit with you a moment?

Sir Wisdom: Sure, sweetie; you two come on in here!

Sir Wisdom: Whew! Look at you, young lady; you're soaking wet! Wait right here!

Sir Wisdom: Here, Tonie, wrap yourself with this towel.

Sir Wisdom: Now what has brought the two of you to my humble abode?

Tonie: Go ahead, Chayi'l. You might as well tell him!

Chayi'l: Sir Wisdom, Tonie and her husband, Derek, have strayed from her original plan of purchasing a small home and gradually building themselves up to several investment properties. She and her husband spoke to me on several occasions about their plans, and I was in awe of their ability to devise a plan to reach their goals.

To my dismay, the two of them have recently moved into a 3,000-square-foot home that cost three times the amount of her original plans. The home is beautiful, of course, but for the entire eight years that they dated, they planned and investigated the real-estate market to understand the dynamics of housing. Now look! They've settled for a thirty-year plan. I guess I shouldn't be upset, but you've taught me that no matter how long you put off the plan, the plan will eventually manifest itself, either through you or through the next generation, but eventually the plan will come to pass.

My prayer is that the plan will include Derek and Antoinette. Please, Mr. Wisdom, can you help me talk to them about their decision, or is it too late? Tell me it's not too late, Mr. Wisdom! Please tell me it's not too late.

You've just completed storyline B**. You are now entering storyline C***

***Hello, my name is Antoinette. Let me provide some facts to the readers about the housing industry of today. But before I do that, let me give you an explanation of how to read and utilize this interactive journal series:

Throughout the beginning of the journal, you will receive simple testimonials and commentaries about housing. Throughout your journey, you will be given basic instructions that you will need to send in to the National HOME Alliance in order to apply for your personal National HOME Alliance homeowner's package.

You must understand that this journal is your entry into your homeowner's package and that it allows the National HOME Alliance committee to determine how best to serve your needs and at which times you need help. So be sure to complete all of the instructions contained within the journal, because it will reveal your character and consistency to abide by rules and regulations, all of which help to determine the necessity of your NHA purchase.

Nearing the end of the journey, you will embrace three storylines that are going on at the same time. These storylines are notated by an asterisk (*) at the beginning of the first storyline and another at the end of it. The second and third are the same, but they are notated with the following: B**, C***.

Now your job is to follow the storylines, which are Tonie and Chayi'l's adventure through their topic.

Do you remember the topic? What is it? _____

_____

During this interactive commentary journal, In storyline B**, you will have an opportunity to hear from Mr. Wisdom's commentary about the bible and how the information it contains is valid for reproof, correction, guidance, grace, and love. Within this commentary, you will find scriptures related to housing or building a foundation.

And finally, Antoinette keeps us updated on today's concerns about the topic of housing and how it affects our todays and our tomorrows within storyline C***. She brings in commentaries and statistics and vital information that will assist the readers in accurately assessing their situations and in making a quality decision about housing now and in the future.

Throughout the pages of each series, you will find Q and A boxes that you are responsible for answering and sending in for analysis at the National HOME Alliance.

The interactive section is very important. Answers to many of your questions, some of your comments, and selected stories will be placed on the forum board pages of each subsequent journal series.

Interaction is imperative. If Antoinette doesn't know that you exist or that your problem is hindering your home life, she can't attempt to help you overcome the obstacles, design a new course of action, or provide a resource that can assist you in overcoming your dilemma. So get involved and adhere to the mentoring of someone who has been there and done that.

Finally, you must follow the course of action (C of A) offered to you. This C of A is the beginning of your healing process and will be sent to you directly from the desk of Antoinette via your coordinator.

The goal is to stay on course. Don't waver or give up. It's not going to be easy. You can't mess up many years of your life and expect to clean up the mess or the nasty consequences that came with the mess overnight.

Remember: your decision yesterday is playing out in your life today, so if you're not ready to change your actions today, then your tomorrow will look the same as your yesterday.

Now, let me relate my personal housing experience to a meal.

Why do I relate this housing situation to a cooked meal?

That's a great question!

Well, here's the answer!

Have you ever been invited to have supper at the Marshalls' house and in the midst of looking forward to going, prepared your appetite to receive a scrumptious, great-tasting meal?

I can just see it! You and your beau got all dolled up. You made sure you didn't eat so that you would have a big appetite.

"Honey, hurry up! We'll be late," you say. Oh! It's going to be a wonderful evening.

Well, you're at the table. The food looks a little funny, but you're still open to try it. The mashed potatoes seem to have big lumps in them, and as you place them on your plate, the creamy, churned, potato splatters away from a huge, hard, semicooked russet that looks as though it has never touched the water.

You take a big gulp and remember that you chose not to eat earlier because of your excitement of the meal.

You continue to serve yourself from the food dishes that are being passed around the table. Soon, the meat dish has passed by.

Well, it looks pretty good, I guess, you say to yourself with an internal sigh. "Mm, mm! Smothered chicken in gravy—my favorite." You take a pretty large piece of the thigh/leg section of the chicken in expectation of providing respite to the salivating glands located in the back of your mouth.

The biscuits come around, and your excitement again excels because of the brown, crusty tops that have dripping butter rolling down the sides. You grab two of them and set them on your plate in anticipation of biting into the buttery, fluffy dough.

And finally, the vegetables have arrived. *Wow!* You declare to your inner being. There is creamed spinach—your ultimate favorite. Boy, are you ready to eat!

You bow your head for Grace, and before the prayer is over, you've grasped the biscuit by the top to add butter to the inside of it. But to your dismay, as you pull the top of the biscuit, it continues to pull. You look down only to discover that the doughy inside has been exposed. The biscuits were not cooked thoroughly enough. What a waste of time, energy, effort, and anticipation you have made for something that looked so promising.

Continuing on around your plate, you grab your fork and knife to dive into the aromatic smell of smothered chicken. You ask Mrs. Marshall about how she prepared the brown mushroom-and-onion gravy that actually tastes pretty good. She tells you that her mother helped her prepare the main course, so you become hopeful that the main dish of the meal is good. You place your fork in the chicken to hold it down and grab your knife and begin to slice off a piece in anticipation. But lo and behold, you see red juices flow down into the plate. Not only is the chicken undercooked, it is literally raw on the inside. You look up in dismay only to see Mr. And Mrs. Marshall enjoying the meal. You decide to discontinue the meal, and you can't understand how the Marshalls are continuing to eat such a meal. You look over at your spouse in disappointing despair. He winks and smiles to assure you that his heart goes out to you. After all is said and done, the meal was just plain ol' nasty!

THE HOUSING TABLE

Suppose, for instance, that you and your husband were in the market to purchase a new home and the realtor explained to you that the house was $670,000 and that your credit would allow you an interest rate of 6.5 percent over a thirty-year fixed term with a down payment of 10 percent of the purchase price totaling $67,000 added to the closing cost of $8000. The full balance just for the down payment sums up to $75,000.

Well, you know that you don't have $75,000 saved up for a down payment, so you tell the realtor to forget the whole deal.

"But wait!" The realtor exclaims.

"We have a program that will allow us to put the $75,000 up for you as a second mortgage, so you can come to the table with no money down."

This 80/20 program is very popular today.

Well, you think that sounds pretty good. "How does that program work?" you ask.

The program sounds promising, and it does allow you to move into the house of your dreams right now!

Let's see. You are given a $595,000 first mortgage at 6.5 percent interest over thirty years and a $75,000 second mortgage at 12 percent over fifteen years. Your first mortgage costs you approximately $3760.99 (PITI) per month, and the second costs you $900.15 per month.

Oh, did I mention that you are a middle-class family with a monthly income of $5,721 per month after taxes?

Oh, I had better mention that you and your wife own two two-year-old vehicles that were purchased while you were living in your apartments, and you still have three years before you pay them off, and your combined payments total $868 per month.

One more thing! You and your wife have accumulated some minor debt with JC Penney, Sears, and Discover for the whopping total of $11,950 with a monthly payment of $230 per month.

By the way, you have 1.5 children. Your daughter is three, and one baby is due in 4.5 months. It's an exciting time for you, and this new house will really set the stage for your new life.

Okay! I just have one more thing to say!

Take the time to go back through the preceding pages and crunch the numbers. The bad news is that your household is at a negative and you haven't even bought groceries yet!

"Why did we move in the first place?" you ask. "Everything looked so promising at the housing table! What was I thinking? It sounded so good a few years ago!"

Or maybe, just maybe, you planned it right, like I did, only to encounter a job loss, medical bills, and a career loss.

Nonetheless, what do we do to be prepared for the next swing of the market?

Will you even be able to afford a home after this buyers' index?

And though it's a buyers' market, your earlier default credit score requires that you place at least 25 percent down in order to get a loan, and your interest rate will be at least 8 to 11 percent.

Is that a good thing or a bad one?

Well, each case is vitally different, and that's where the National HOME Alliance comes in. We need you to be a successful homeowner if our state is to maintain the status quo of being a powerhouse state of opportunity. So keep focus, and let's figure out how to get you back in the Olympic Game of housing.

What do you mean by Olympic Game of Housing?

Let me now refer to the housing industry from a sports perspective.

Yes! I said sports! But first let's take a blast through the past!

As I embark with you through this journey of housing and homeownership, I bring you updated information and statistics that may affect you now and in the future. As we are all aware, the decisions of yesterday have greater effect on the buyer today. Today it is becoming more and more difficult to buy property and to obtain the American dream of homeownership.

The current housing prices have been excruciating to the middle-class sector, and what I have noticed is that the once middle-ground (middle class) citizens are being pushed up or pushed down into a high-class sect or into a low-class sect.

It is unfortunate that the median housing cost in the inland empire is approximately $375,000. Pretty soon we will notice that the once affordable inland empire will outprice the middle-class buyer.

A BLAST THROUGH THE PAST

In 1985, a family that made $36,000 per year between the husband and wife could live comfortably in a new home of $86,000. With an interest rate of 8 percent, a family would have a mortgage of approximately $688. With two cars (even if new), a payment would estimate out at $519 for a total of $1,207. Groceries averaged about $250 for a family of four per month, and utilities were just a fraction of $100 (except in the summer). A household of four had a base take-home income of $2,250 per month and would have an approximate monthly debt of $1,757 with tithes and offerings, activities, and extra spending, leaving a balance of $273 per month for saving.

Let's talk vehicles for a moment:

As you drove down the street, you didn't see many brand-new cars or used cars for that matter. The family of the '80s would keep their cars and pass them down to the next generation. I should know. The first car given to me was a 1964 Datsun four-door. I never did get that thing running. My first purchase was a 1973 Honda Accord hatchback, and I didn't buy based upon the look; I purchased based upon the feasibility of paying on the vehicle until it was paid off.

Today's family will purchase a new car for upwards of $30,000 every three to five years because they need the image to coincide with their fluctuating business income.

Time out: Let me explain to you what happened to me back in 1997 when I first started researching for this company. A good friend of mine had taken her company from nothing to something in about three years. She went from zero to millions in that time. She owned an insurance company and obtained many contracts with the state and surrounding counties. She would often explain to me that I needed to rent or lease a Mercedes in order to hobnob with the bigwigs. I inquired as to why I needed to be so dramatic. She explained that rich people only help rich people. She said that many times, she was invited to attend shindigs for rich people and would have to rent vehicles and lease jewelry and clothing in order to fit in. She reiterated that that was how she obtained the majority of her contracts.

After much debate, I decided that this was not something that I could or would be interesting in doing. She asked why. I merely stated, "Where are those friends today, now that you no longer have this business?" We did not speakof the façade of fitting in from that point on.

Now, why did I go through all of that information?

Are you living in a façade?

Why do you drive the car that you drive? Does it fit into your budget, or does your budget fit into it?

Are you avoiding the truth that you are living above and beyond your means, or are you so close to the means that if one hiccup occurs, you will surrender all, and it won't be to the Lord?

Is this your storyline?

The payments for new vehicles are running upwards of $621 per month per vehicle, and each family has one new car for the wife and one new or used car for the husband. These normally cost $10,000 to $15,000 for a payment of $340 per month, and God forbid if teenagers are in the picture, which most often is the case. Let's take a look at the final numbers.

The cost of the vehicles, the high cost gas prices due to the long commute, and tune-ups, oil changes, tires and registration add up, and don't even mention the cost of insurance. Well, let's give you the benefit of the doubt by saying that your vehicle expenses total $1,500 per month. And you and your wife are doing pleasingly well with a whopping $7,200 take-home payment per month. Congratulations on a good income, because today's median take-home income is at approximately $5,241.66.

Okay, $7200-$1500 = **$5700**

Well that looks pretty good, doesn't it! I would say so!

Let us continue.

You purchased a home in Corona or Temecula in 2004 for $375,000. Your monthly payment was only $2,437 with an excellent interest rate of 6.5% percent. Let's do the numbers.

Okay $5700-$2437 = **$3263**

Your family is still thriving above the norm, and I'm proud of you for that, but let's continue on with the scenario of the average family. It would be perfect if we could stop right here and call it a day, but we can't.

Did you ask why?

Well I'm gonna tell you, but you didn't hear it from me!

I forgot to mention that because the model home was so beautiful and you wanted your house to be decorated just like it, you decided to take out a second mortgage and upgrade your home and refurnish it. (Some families just upgrade it and add it to the purchase of the home. Some families will use it to pay off the credit card debt that they accumulated while fixing up the home. Still others add a swanky, top-of-the-line backyard that is designed for the best parties and functions.)

What did you use your second mortgage for?

Do you have a second mortgage on your home?

Did you know that your equity should be used for making more money by using it for things like investing purposes?

Were you aware that equity should never be considered a savings account with which to spend and buy more, because you are not mandated to replace your savings account, but you are required to pay back a second mortgage? Therefore, if your second mortgage is not bringing in an income, then you have created another taxable debt that may or may not depreciate in the future.

But you didn't hear it from me!

Let's continue with the equity line.

Well, most second mortgage are for today's average equity of $175,000. Remember: the house is now worth $550,000. $375,000 was the original purchase price, so you now have $175,000 in equity. Now the second mortgage, of course comes at the high price of 13.5 percent for a new payment of $2,275 per month.

Now let's crunch the numbers again to see where our family is at.

Where was it? Where was the last okay? Did you find it? Tell me where it was? Oh yeah! I found it.

Okay, $3263-$2275 = **$988.00**

Do you still feel excited?

Well, to tell you the truth, if that were the final straw and there were no more straw to burn, then I guess I would still congratulate you. But we never added the cost of food, clothing, entertainment, activities, the mall, the mall, the mall, the movies, the cinema, or Edwards, or AMC…you get my drift.

You see, there are many of us who would continue to live in denial and smile like the man on the commercial who says he's up to his eyeballs in debt and begs for someone to help him.

Avoiding the situation and denying the truth will ultimately lead to nasty consequences, just like that meal with the Marshalls (and by the way, this is just a ficticious name).

Oh! Don't think that I'm judging you, because I've been there and done that. I've failed more times than one. I believe I've earned the right to speak to you frankly and openly about housing and the consequences that may or may not come with it. I believe that the

Wisdom that has come from mistake after mistake after mistake, has not only led to my success, but has allowed me to Mentor you.

Who better to here from than someone who has not only been where you are today, but who has overcome and found success in the truth. I'm inviting you to come with me. Yes! Come with me. Relearn success and stay focused on how to really have the "American Dream."

Now I know your situation is not like everyone else's or is it?

Can you relate to this storyline or do you know someone who can?

Mom or Dad, Aunt Ida, or Mr. Paxton, who do you know that needs to hear this word?

Please! Stop now!

Go to the question and answer section and complete it and send it in. This may be the most important day of your entire life, I need to hear your story and I desire to help you overcome the obstacles and rediscovery of reaching your goals the right way.

I'm thankful for your beginning this journey with me into the depths of housing and homelessness. Though many of you may never taste what I have tasted or possibly some of you have, I want to help you. Allow me to partner up with you and assist you in being an overcomer in housing.

Oh! Don't even get the idea that I'm here to bail you out of your current situation, because I'm not here for that. But I am here to walk with those who want to walk right. I know it won't be an easy walk, but my presence may make it easier to accomplish the cleanup task.

Also, along the journey's way, the Lord may instruct me to bless those that He has chosen to receive from Him, so stay focused and pray diligently you may be the chosen one.

The following pages are designed for you to journal your feelings, concerns and possible solutions to your current situation. Dig deep into the caverns of your mind and I'm sure hidden behind the hurt, embarrassment, pain and exhaustion, you'll find the answers to your problem.

And most importantly, Follow your first mind! At all cost. Stay stable no matter how long the journey may seem to go.

_____
_____
_____
_____
_____
_____
_____
_____
_____
_____
_____
_____
_____
_____
_____
_____
_____
_____
_____
_____
_____
_____
_____

Congratulations! You have just completed your stability course in housing. Send in your information and you will receive your personal invitation to a graduation dinner offered only to the members who have completed this first journal series.

At the dinner, you will have the opportunity to hear from Antoinette and receive a signed copy of the next journal. You will also hear valuable insights about understanding the dynamics of housing.

Come and join us as we provide viable options to current housing woes and insight to families on how to maintain an income status that can propel them to their next level in housing.

Most importantly, come because it is at no cost to you. Yes! I said the dinner is on me! I would like to get to know you and ask you some questions about the journal and your personal journey. So I'll see you soon! RSVP as soon as faithfully possible (ASAFP)!

I love you in the Lord! Stay focused! You'll be home soon.